GAME
WARDEN

GAME WARDEN

Adventures of a Wildlife Warrior

By

William Wasserman

GAME WARDEN

Adventures of a Wildlife Warrior

By

William Wasserman

Other books by William Wasserman
Poacher Wars
The Best of It's a Wild Life
Pennsylvania Wildlife Tails
More Pennsylvania Wildlife Tails

Copyright © 2010 by Penn's Woods Publications

A Penn's Woods Book

ISBN 0-9718907-7-3

Cover by John Wasserman

For John,
game warden
brother
friend

Introduction

As a Wildlife Conservation Officer for more than three decades, I investigated thousands of game law violations throughout the Commonwealth of Pennsylvania.

While many believe the majority of poaching incidents are perpetrated by some downtrodden, poverty-stricken individual simply trying to put meat on his table, truth is, most poachers drive expensive vehicles, possess criminal records, and poach wildlife with high-priced firearms equipped with costly night-vision scopes and illegal silencers. They kill for greed, money, bragging rights, or for the sheer lunacy of simply watching an animal die, only to leave it rotting.

Having spent more than half my life tracking down and arresting outlaw hunters, I wrote this book so folks will have a better understanding of what it's like to be part of the thin green line of dedicated wildlife warriors, commonly called game wardens, who risk their lives daily in order to protect our natural resources.

The incidents recounted in this book are real; however, the stories are based on my memories over a period of years and may differ from the memories of others. I admit to taking some creative liberties with events and to re-creating some of the dialog. I have also given the poachers and their associates fictitious names and have altered their physical descriptions. Any resemblance to actual persons, living or dead is entirely coincidental.

The woods are lovely, dark and deep.
But I have promises to keep,
And miles to go before I sleep,
And miles to go before I sleep.
— Robert Frost

It is eternity now. I am in the midst of it. It is about me in the sunshine...

— Richard Jefferies

In Broad Daylight

W HEN THE SHOT rang out, Dakota Blue had just taken a bite out of a freshly made ham sandwich, but now his stomach tightened into a sickening knot.

Laying his lunch on the table, he grabbed his binoculars off the counter and shuffled to the kitchen window to scan the woods behind his house. Although squirrel season was open, Dakota Blue had a sneaking suspicion that somebody was after much bigger game.

It had been a shotgun blast, of that he was certain, and as he moved his eyepiece slowly across the dim tree line, his gaze settled on an indistinct bobbing movement deep in the woods. He fingered the dial on his binoculars, zooming in quickly, and the shadowy form suddenly materialized into the silhouette of a man — a man that he recognized instantly. He was hunkered behind a rotting log, hitching a large hunting knife though the bloodied sternum of a deer.

When Limping Wolf finished gutting the carcass, he wiped his heavy blade on his jeans and slid it into a leather sheath. Then he stood from the low shadow into the abounding daylight, his bronze face and shoulder-length raven hair glistening in the warm midday sun. He was six foot three, lean and sinewy. His imposing stature, coupled with his broad forehead, high cheekbones and peculiarly flattened nose, was unmistakable even from afar.

Dakota Blue watched intently as Limping Wolf shouldered his drag rope and leaned into it with a great, jubilant smile. The deer, a buck, weighed well over 100 pounds, but Limping Wolf dragged the carcass behind him as if it were no more than a rag doll. And as he stole through the shadowed forest, he congratulated himself on his cleverness: It was Friday afternoon, a workday for his unsuspecting neighbor. And unless he stumbled upon the gut pile before the coyotes got to it — extremely unlikely since Dakota Blue seldom ventured past the mowed portion of his yard — he would never know the deer had been taken.

Had it been any other afternoon that particular week, Limping Wolf would have been right. Dakota Blue never missed a day at his desk in town. But feeling a bit under the weather, he had taken an uncustomary day off. And that decision would ultimately spell disaster for Limping Wolf and his clan.

Outraged by what he had witnessed, Dakota Blue slipped out of his house and began to follow Limping Wolf through the woods until he reached his property line a quarter mile away. Here he crouched low and watched him drag the buck across his unkempt lawn to an open barn door. From the barn, another man walked out to greet him: Fast Hand Jon.

Fast Hand, as always, was armed — a holstered Smith & Wesson revolver plainly visible on his hip. Thin and boney with a long scrawny neck, his gaping eyes bulged from their sockets at the sight of Limping Wolf. The two men clasped palms briefly, then Fast Hand grabbed the drag rope and ran it through a pulley atop the doorway. Both men hoisted the deer until it dangled just off the ground, and while Fast Hand secured the rope, Limping Wolf pulled his razor-sharp blade and prepared to skin the carcass.

In more than 30 years as a state game warden, I could count on one hand the number of occasions I had received information as timely as the voice on the phone telling me about Limping Wolf and Fast Hand Jon. If I hurried, I could catch them red-handed, he told me. I thanked Dakota Blue for the information and hung up. It would be a short jaunt, less than 10 miles, and I wanted to get there before anyone disposed of the carcass.

The narrow dirt lane leading to Limping Wolf's property seemed endless. It was uphill all the way, and my Ford gobbled the distance greedily as I bounced over gaping potholes and exposed bedrock. Rounding a sharp bend, I noticed a dilapidated barn to my immediate right. It sat parallel to my vehicle, obscuring my view, and when I broke past it I suddenly spotted two men in the clearing before me.

For a moment, time stood still, the blazing sun shining vividly upon stunned faces. Caught in mid-stride, both men stood woodenly in the tall grass, eyes wide open at the sight of my approaching vehicle. They were surrounded by a jungle of broken farm equipment and odd junk. An ancient Chevy pickup squatted on a broken frame behind them, its faded body rotting from decades outdoors. At least a dozen 55-gallon drums were scattered haphazardly about the property, many of them capsized and coated with rust. I zeroed in on Fast Hand. He was covered with blood, a holstered six-shooter on his belt. And as my marked patrol vehicle slid to a stop in the loose gravel, he turned and began to run.

Out the door in an instant, I took cover behind the front fender and commanded him to halt. Fast Hand froze in his tracks. Then, without warning, he spun toward me, his left hand dropping toward his gun.

I unsnapped my holster and drew my Glock before he broke leather, and realized instantly that I'd beaten him only because he pulled back at the last second.

"PUT YOUR HANDS IN THE AIR!" I cried.

Fast Hand raised both palms high. I shouted for Limping

Wolf to do the same. He complied immediately, exposing the wicked Bowie knife strapped to his belt. Although I had a clear advantage at this point, I approached the two armed poachers with great caution. And because my eyes were locked so intently upon them, I almost missed their partner as I crossed in front of the barn. An arm's thrust away, someone stood behind the half-skinned carcass of a deer hanging in the open doorway. I spotted her from the corner of my eye. Short and stout, a bloody skinning knife clenched in her fist.

My heart jumped as I wheeled to face her. "Drop the knife and step out, now!" I commanded while backing away. The blade fell from her hand, her stony face staring at me as she slid from behind the deer. Suddenly I felt surrounded. Almost overwhelmed. *What next? Someone taking potshots at me from behind a tree . . . ?*

Ordering her to stand with the two men, I picked up her folding knife and dropped it into my pocket. Next, I told Fast Hand to lace his fingers behind his head and drop to his knees. He obeyed and slowly crouched into a kneeling position in the grass. Stepping behind him, I retrieved his .38 revolver from its holster, stuck it in my belt, and frisked him for additional weapons while keeping a guarded eye on Limping Wolf and the woman. Satisfied he was clean, I had Fast Hand lay belly-down on the ground before turning to face Limping Wolf.

He looked wired. Crazy. His eyes dancing wildly in his head, lips twitching nervously. A thin white scar zigzagged across his left cheek from the corner of his eye down to his broad chin. *An old knife wound, perhaps*, I thought.

"Just keep your hands in the air," I said calmly. He glanced at the woman. His expression menacing, like an angry pit bull waiting to be launched. She gave him a hard look and a subtle headshake. Her message clear: *Don't even think about it!*

I nodded approvingly at her and ordered Limping Wolf to unbuckle his belt with his left hand and let it drop to the ground with his knife. The woman must have had a strong influence on him, for his face had softened now, his eyes strangely vacant as he unsnapped his belt and let it fall. I had him kick it aside, and then directed him to lie on his belly facing away from it. He did this, his expression emotionless.

I looked at the woman. She bowed her head in despair. "We won't give you no trouble, officer," she moaned. "My boys don't mean you no harm. You're just doing your job. I understand."

Holstering my gun, I said, "Everybody stay where you are and we'll get along just fine." I unsnapped my portable radio from my belt, keyed the mike, and called for backup.

Game Warden Mark Rutkowski's voice came back to me: *"Car five-two-three responding. Where are you, Bill?"*

Rutkowski was close by. I gave my location and within minutes heard his patrol car churning up the gravel lane. He parked next to my vehicle and hustled over. "Bill . . . are you okay?"

"Yeah, I'm fine," I said. "Just ran into some folks who wanted to rush the season a little." Rutkowski was a good 20 years younger then me, but he was plenty experienced, and someone you could count on when things got tough. I explained what had happened and asked him to keep an eye on my three suspects while I searched the barn. "Got a strange feeling someone is watching us."

Rutkowski nodded. "No problem, Bill."

I looked at the woman. She'd been eyeing us with keen interest. "Is this your property?"

"Yes, sir, and there's another deer cut up inside that tub," she said pointing a stubby finger toward a large plastic container 50 feet away. "You already seen the one hanging at the barn. Just the two of them, that's all we got. But go ahead and look around if you want to. Won't find nothing, but you're welcome to look."

I glanced at the tub. From where I stood, it was impossible to see inside. "Buck or doe?"

"Doe," she said, shaking her head with regret. "A fine, plump doe."

I frowned in pathetic disapproval as I considered how

many deer these folks must have killed over the years. "What's inside the barn?"

The woman grinned a gummy, toothless smile. "A bunch of worthless junk! Same as you see out here." She paused for a moment, eyeing me up and down. Then said, "Plenty of spiders and rats too. Watch your step if you're going inside."

My face wrinkled with loathing, which prompted Rutkowski to peer at me with a sidelong grin. "I'll go!" he said in an enthusiastic voice.

I returned a lame smile. "No. I'll go. It's my case; you stay here and cover me."

"It's the rats, huh?" he whispered. "I hate 'em too."

I shook my head. "It's not the rats — it's spiders. I can't stand them! Rats will run from you every time. But spiders just hang there and let you walk right into them . . . gives me the creeps just thinking about it." I paused for a moment and gave Rutkowski a hard look. "But that's between us girls, okay?"

Rutkowski glanced at the barn and back to me. "I had a tarantula for a pet once," he said with a straight face. "Big hairy sucker. We got along just fine. Sure you don't want me to go?"

"I'd rather take a bullet! Now, if you could stop snickering long enough to cover me, I'm going in."

Rutkowski knew my run-in with Limping Wolf and his clan had stressed me out, and he'd managed to play me just long enough to get my mind focused on the barn where it belonged. The fact dawned on me quite suddenly as I glanced his way one last time before moving out. He was different now; his face hard and determined. He nodded solemnly at me, "Got your back, brother."

"I know," I said.

Slipping cautiously into the unlit barn, Glock at the ready, I couldn't help wondering if someone might be hiding behind a dark corner waiting to put a bullet in my brain. That grim notion, coupled with the image of some big hairy spider crouching in the dark with its long segmented legs groping

16

for me, made my skin start to crawl as I inched along the dirt floor. I swept my flashlight across the barn's perimeter. The building was split into three stalls, each strewn with an assortment of discarded junk and ancient farm machinery. I watched a portly rat skitter under a discarded hunk of scrap metal. The only sign of life. By the looks of things, no one had been inside the building for years.

Stepping back outside, I squinted into the sun and stood alongside Rutkowski. "Barn's clear," I said. "Let's take a look at the tub."

After discovering the quartered remains of a second deer inside — it was a doe, just as the woman had said — I told Limping Wolf and Fast Hand to get to their feet.

Both men stood and brushed themselves off. "That's all we got, officer," said Fast Hand, "just the two deer."

"Who killed them?"

Limping Wolf hooked two thumbs into his belt loops and rocked on his feet. "I shot both of them. Got one yesterday and one today. Killed them with a rifled slug — a twelve-gauge." He paused, his eyes narrowing sharply. "How'd *you* find out about it?"

"Anyone else on the property?" I asked, ignoring his question.

"Pop's up at the house," Limping Wolf said with a sly grin. "He's probably watching us right now!"

Rutkowski glanced over his shoulder and I watched the corners of his mouth draw down. There was a shabby doublewide trailer 200 feet behind us, and I shuddered with the icy realization that we were within easy range of anyone wanting to pick us off.

"I'm going up there," I said to my partner. "Keep our friends company until I get back." Rutkowski nodded and covered me while I moved cautiously toward the trailer using our patrol cars and a few big trees as shields along the way. I reckoned we would have been shot long ago if anyone had a mind to, and I kept telling myself that over and over again as I crept forward.

Finally, through the screened front door, I could see a

figure sitting in a wheelchair. An older man, and he motioned me in. He had a plastic mask on his face, an oxygen tank behind him, his breathing shallow and labored.

I opened the door, stepped into a disheveled, narrow kitchen, and discovered that the man had been watching us through a wide picture window the whole time. "State Game Commission," I announced. "Relax, sir, everything is going to be okay." The man looked up at me with hooded eyes and nodded once. A scoped .22 caliber rifle leaned in a corner within easy reach of him. I stepped closer. "Is that loaded?"

He nodded again: a weary, forlorn kind of nod. A nod that told me he intended no harm. "I'm going to take the gun and unload it, sir," I told him. And I watched a tear trickle down the white stubble on his unshaven cheek as I picked up the rifle, emptied it, and dumped the bullets into my pocket. "Do you need medical attention, an ambulance or anything?" I asked.

He shook his head, telling me he did not, and I walked out of the trailer and back down to the barn. Everyone looked surprised when they saw the rifle in my hands, including Limping Wolf. "Someone needs to check on Pop," I said to all three suspects at once. "He seems upset."

"I better go up," the woman said gravely. "Is that all right?"

"Go," I said. "If he needs help let us know immediately."

She hustled toward the house wringing her wrists nervously, her eyes thanking me as she passed. I nodded in reply and turned my attention to the two men. "Couldn't wait until the season opened, huh?"

Limping Wolf blew out a long, whistling sigh. "Look around," he gestured with his hand. "We got nothing. No jobs. No money. Nothing. I shot the deer for food, man. Gotta do something until we can find work again."

Rutkowski shook his head with disapproval. "If you want deer meat, we can get you plenty of it. You don't have to do this!"

Limping Wolf looked stunned. "Say what?"

18

"Road kills, mistake kills, we get them all the time. All you had to do was ask."

Both men stared back in genuine surprise. "You serious?" exclaimed Fast Hand Jon.

"Give us a call, we'll put you on the list," I said. "But right now we have to deal with the two deer you have here today. At $500 per animal, you're looking at a $1000 fine for each person involved — and there were three of you."

Limping Wolf bristled at the news. "But *I* killed them, why should anyone else be fined?"

"Because they assisted you in the commission of a crime," I said. "Poaching is illegal. Anyone who helps you with an unlawfully killed deer is subject to the same penalty as you are."

He opened his mouth to speak but stopped cold when something caught his attention behind me. Glancing over my shoulder, I saw the woman approaching hurriedly from the trailer. She smiled and waved a fleshy arm, her bloody apron flopping left and right across her knees as she waddled toward us. "Pop is okay!" she called out. "He's gonna be okay!"

After directing her to stand with Limping Wolf and Fast Hand, I told her about the penalties they were facing. She stared back at me in stunned silence, her mouth forming a perfect O of surprise.

"But, sir," she gasped, "we don't have that kind of money — and I can't go to jail! Pop needs me here with him."

I glanced at Rutkowski. He gave me a subtle, hopeless shrug; his expression foretelling the empathy he felt for the woman and the elderly man she cared for. I was relieved to see it too, because visions of the disabled man, his eyes brimming with tears, haunted me as I struggled with my decision whether or not to confiscate the deer. If I let them keep the venison, it would only be the second time in 30 years that I allowed anyone to possess a deer they killed unlawfully.

I had learned long ago that most poachers shoot deer

either for their trophy antlers or simply as target practice. In the course of my career, I had come across hundreds that had been shot dead and left to rot. Trophy bucks would be skull-capped, brains oozing from their heads, so that some sicko could run off with the "horns" and brag about them to his friends. But it wasn't just trophy deer that were killed. After all, *buck or doe, down they go,* is the poacher's sad dictum. And believe me, there is nothing more revolting than to find a pregnant doe lying dead in a field along some back road to nowhere with twins or triplets in her belly.

However, that wasn't the case here. Nor was it an excuse, because people don't starve in America, they don't have to poach game in order to survive. But I also knew that some folks are too proud to ask for handouts, and thought that might be the case with Limping Wolf and Fast Hand Jon.

In truth, I had decided not to prosecute the woman long ago. But the two men would have to be dealt with even though it sickened me when I considered how it would impact the woman and the old man. Part of me wanted to simply walk away, just turn my back and forget I ever saw them. But that was impossible. And although I didn't believe for a single moment that a fine would keep Limping Wolf or Fast Hand Jon from poaching in the future, I wasn't about to let them off scot-free.

Still, I didn't have to take the deer. After all, if anyone looked like they needed a handout, these people certainly did. But if word got out about it, as it so often does in the backcountry, it could give the impression of weakness on my part. And I needed to come up with a way to prevent that from happening.

So, with the above in mind, I turned and motioned for Rutkowski to follow me to my patrol car. Then, while keeping a cautious eye on our three suspects, I spoke in a low voice: "I've decided not to take the deer."

Rutkowski regarded me for a long moment, then he rolled his eyes and nodded shrewdly. "I see . . . it's the old man and the woman, right?"

"Yes," I said. "It would be like taking food from a baby, for crying out loud! And I'm not going to do that." I glanced over his shoulder at our captive trio. "We'll take photographs of the deer for evidence, and just let 'em keep the meat."

Rutkowski rubbed his chin contemplatively and stared at me. Then I watched his expression slowly melt into a comprehending smile.

"*What . . . ?*" I said stiffly.

"Nothing," he shrugged. "I'll probably get like that too some day."

"Get like what?"

"You know . . . a bit long in my career, feeling more generous, kindhearted . . . that sort of thing."

"Kindhearted? I'm not *kindhearted!*"

Rutkowski eyed me with a face of stone. "Oh . . . ?"

His reaction confounded me, and I suddenly felt compelled to defend myself: ". . . Besides, the deer are all cut up. We'll have to run all over town trying to find something to put all the blood-soaked pieces into, and then drive 20 miles back to headquarters just so we can store everything in the evidence freezer!"

Rutkowski cocked his head and broke into a thin, mischievous smile. He had me once again, and I shook my head in dazed resignation. My expression only added to his amusement, and his shoulders begin to tremble as he stifled the laughter welling up inside him.

I shrugged and let out a soft chuckle. "Am I that easy, or do you do this to everyone?"

"Mostly just you," he grinned.

"Then you're okay with letting them keep the deer?"

"Yes, for the old man and the woman . . . I'm okay with it."

We returned to our suspects. "Two men, two deer, two thousand dollars," I said flatly. I paused to give them a moment for my statement sink in. "The woman walks away free — that is, as long as you two agree to plead guilty and pay your fines."

Limping Wolf's expression grew dark and predatory. He

swung his head sharply toward the woman, his long black hair reflecting jagged glints of light in the sun. She glared back at him, and I watched his grim face flinch into weary submission.

"But, officer," she said sadly, "we don't have that kind of money."

"I understand that, ma'am. But it's the minimum fine for poaching two deer in this state. Ask the judge to give your boys time-payments; as long as they don't fall behind, they won't go to jail."

"Yes, sir," she replied. "I guess that means you'll be taking the deer too."

I glanced at Rutkowski; his young, vital face had drawn into an expression of genuine compassion for the woman. "Actually," I said, "my partner talked me into letting you keep the deer."

Rutkowski snapped out of his empathetic trance and stared at me in wide-eyed amazement. He whipped his head toward the woman. She was ogling him in gleeful appreciation.

"Well, aren't you a fine young man!" she beamed.

"Yes, he certainly is!" I crowed. "It was his idea not to prosecute you, either, ma'am. He convinced me of that while we were back at my truck a moment ago."

Limping Wolf and Fast Hand Jon looked on in open astonishment as the woman fluttered her eyes at Rutkowski. I almost cracked a rib trying to keep a straight face.

My Good cop/Bad cop ploy had worked, but seeing the woman couldn't take her eyes off my partner, I thought I'd better bail him out.

"Ma'am!" I barked.

She released Rutkowski from her dreamy stare, and gawked at me. "Officer . . .?"

"My partner doesn't want you prosecuted because he feels sorry for Pop, not you."

The woman glanced at Rutkowski and he nodded in tight-lipped agreement.

I turned to Limping Wolf and Fast Hand Jon. "Citations

will be coming in the mail. Make sure you contact the judge as soon as they arrive, otherwise, warrants will be issued for your arrest."

Later that afternoon, as Rutkowski and I sat over coffee and paperwork at a restaurant in downtown Tunkhannock, I thanked him for backing me up.

"Pick up the tab and we're even!" he winked.

I sipped my coffee and smiled over the cup. "I'll call you if I get arrest warrants on our boys. Give you a chance to see your girlfriend again."

Rutkowski chuckled at the notion, and I laughed along with him. It had been a good day with a good friend, and I was glad for it.

The incident with Limping Wolf and Fast Hand Jon came to a successful conclusion that day. Both men were charged with hunting deer in closed season, and eventually paid off their fines. They also lost their hunting and trapping privileges for three years, but since they never owned hunting licenses, it wouldn't have affected them much. And although Limping Wolf had assured us that he and Fast Hand would be in touch the next time they needed meat, Rutkowski and I never heard from either of them again.

An attitude not only of defense, but defiance.
                                        —Thomas Gillespie

CUDA

HIS **SPOTLIGHT** pierced the crisp night air like a laser as Junior Child swept its beam across the orchard. He and his cousin Lew had been driving through the backcountry for hours in search of a 10-point buck they'd been hearing rumors about, and they were beginning to doubt its existence when Junior suddenly spotted the animal with a small herd of deer.

"Wow! Look at the size of that rack!"

Lew gazed at the buck in utter disbelief as it browsed with impunity amid the abundant apple trees. It was a giant. Its heavy antlers unusually thick and wide, even for a deer of such tremendous weight. He had seen big whitetails before, but nothing like this; it dwarfed the other deer as they fed among the fallen apples. "I know where *I'm* hunting next week!" beamed Lew.

"You mean where *we're* hunting," Junior shot back. He was eyeing the buck eagerly.

Lew glanced at his cousin, then back at the deer. "Knew you were gonna say that," he chuckled.

"This is Jimmy Mexico's property," said Junior. "He works at the mill with my father. They're pretty tight, too. I think he'll give us permission to hunt here if we ask."

"Awesome!" cried Lew. "Then we won't have to sneak in."

Junior whipped his head toward his cousin, his eyes like wounding darts. "I ain't no poacher! We get permission or we don't hunt here. Period!"

"Okay! Okay," shrugged Lew. "Let's just hope your father comes through for us. I'd hate to see someone else get this monster before we do."

The sudden lights of an oncoming vehicle caused them to turn heads. They watched as it began to slow to a crawl and then pull to the berm behind them. Next, the lights went dead and the engine shut down, leaving the mysterious vehicle squatting silently in the dark.

"Who the heck is that?" grumbled Lew. "They're gonna spook the deer!"

Junior saw a vanity tag on the front bumper that said "CUDA" in large silver letters, and recognized the nickname instantly. He could see two men sitting inside a Chevrolet sedan. The driver was Lonnie McNabb. Roscoe Coon sat alongside him. He had graduated high school with both of them just last year.

Holding his spotlight on the deer, Junior pulled his upper body halfway out the passenger window and waved excitedly at the two men. But his smile transformed into a look of horror when he saw Roscoe point the barrel of a .30 caliber rifle out his window and take aim.

There was no time to react. The gun discharged a thunderous roar, its muzzle spewing a jagged yellow flame into the night. Junior stared in utter disbelief as the band of terrified deer began to scatter through the trees. But the giant 10-point buck lagged behind. Struck directly through the heart it staggered sideways and collapsed.

Junior cast his light directly into the Chevrolet's windshield, blinding the occupants. *"Are you crazy!"* he roared.

Roscoe Coon made a vulgar gesture with his hand and pulled his rifle back inside. Then the sedan rumbled to life and sped past their car, leaving them in a choking wake of road dust as it went by.

"Get in!" hollered Lew. "We're going after them!"

Junior dropped back into his seat and Lew decked the accelerator, his rear tires spewing gravel into the orchard as he shot forward.

The narrow dirt lane was difficult enough to negotiate in daylight. Darkness made driving almost impossible. Still, Lew was gaining on them until the road became covered with a blinding curtain of dust from the fleeing vehicle, forcing him to back off or risk running into a tree.

"Watch where they go when they hit the hard road!" Lew barked, slamming on his brakes. "It's just ahead."

Junior saw the sedan pull onto the macadam and disappear into the night. "They turned left!" he cried. "Looks like they're heading toward McNabb's house."

Lew tightened his fingers around the steering wheel and turned toward Junior. "Good! Now that we know where to find them, we gotta get to a phone!"

It's unusual to hear from someone who can not only identify a poacher, but who is also eager to testify against that person in a court of law. Lew and Junior told me they were willing to do just that, and agreed to see me within the hour.

I wanted to question the suspects as soon as possible, and arranged to meet my two witnesses, along with one of my deputies, at the state police barracks for a quick huddle. As I listened to their incredible story, my interest grew. The fact that they were innocently shining a deer when two men pulled up behind them and shot it dead, right out from under their spotlight, astounded me. Why would anybody commit a flagrant act of poaching in plain view of someone they knew? Someone who could put the finger on them? It didn't make sense, and I was anxious to pay these men a visit.

The poachers lived about 10 miles apart in Lemon Township. Lew and Junior knew where their homes were, and volunteered to guide us to them, so we decided to split up — my deputy going to Roscoe Coon's place with Lew, while Junior and I proceeded to Lonnie McNabb's house.

It was just past midnight when I eased my patrol car down McNabb's dirt driveway and killed the lights. He must have been expecting me, too, because he hurried out the front door and came striding toward my vehicle as I stepped out.

The moon cast a pale light upon his frame as he strode forward, allowing me the ability to see if he reached for a hidden gun as I stood by my front fender for cover.

"State game warden!" I announced as he approached.

He stopped and stuffed both hands deep into his pockets. "What's up?" he asked with feigned cordiality.

The temperature had dropped into the low thirties, and a million stars winked down at us like sparkling diamonds in the sky. My coat was zipped, but McNabb wore only a T-shirt and jeans. He was 19 years old and medium height with a stocky, muscular build. He wore his hair in a neat buzz-cut, and I reckoned he'd been a wrestler or a football player in school.

"I'm here about the deer that you and Roscoe Coon shot tonight," I said.

McNabb never flinched at my accusation. "Deer? We didn't shoot any deer!"

"No?" I replied mockingly. "Then I must be at the wrong house. Aren't you Lonnie McNabb?"

"Cuda."

"Say what?"

"Call me Cuda; I hate the name Lonnie. And I don't know anything about no deer."

"Is that right?" I said. "Well, I want you to meet someone who thinks differently."

Junior had told me earlier that he was willing to confront McNabb that night if necessary, and I agreed to let him — but not without some reservations. Face-to-face accusations between a suspect and witness can quickly deteriorate into a hostile situation, and I had warned Junior to keep his distance when he engaged McNabb.

Sitting in the back seat of my darkened patrol vehicle, he had managed to remain undetected. But now the door swung open and he jumped out. "I saw you do it, Cuda!" he cried. "It was wrong, and I'm not going to let this go. You were driving and Roscoe shot the deer. It's not right!"

Lonnie McNabb stared into his accuser's eyes and shook his head coolly. "Wasn't me," he said.

McNabb had an icy air of indifference about him that hit you like an arctic blast. *Wasn't me!* I thought. *What kind of an answer was that?*

Most people simply do not respond to an accusation that way. An innocent man would have come back with an indignant denial proclaiming his innocence — and be deeply troubled by the charge. And even a guilty person generally comes up with an alibi or an excuse — or at the very least, a good old-fashioned lie: *I was watching TV with my girlfriend; I was asleep at home; I didn't do it, but I know who did* — something!

But *wasn't me* just didn't cut it. Not when an eyewitness is pointing a stern finger of guilt right at you. Not when The Warden is eyeing you with I-know-you-did-it written all over his hardened face — and most certainly, not when you're only nineteen years old. Where was the respect for the law that young people had when I was growing up? Had it eroded this far?

Junior stared back at McNabb as if he'd been slapped in the face. "But I was right there!" he cried. "I saw you, and you know it. You're a *liar*, McNabb!"

But the iceman simply shrugged his heavy shoulders, his expression both impassive and unmoving.

Junior continued to glare at McNabb for a moment. Then he turned to me with a puzzled look that screamed, *Now what?* I quickly raised my palm and motioned for him to back off.

I looked over at McNabb's closed garage door. "You drive a Chevy sedan, don't you?"

"Yeah," he shrugged.

"Mind if I take a look at it?"

"Yeah, I do."

I couldn't believe this kid. "Look," I said, "we can play it the hard way or the easy way. It'll take me about an hour to get a search warrant (In truth, it probably would have taken half the night, but I knew I'd get one eventually.). But the warrant won't just be for your car. It'll be for your garage, your barn, your house, everything — right down to your underwear drawer."

The idea seemed to put a crack in Lonnie McNabb's invisible suit of armor, for he immediately did an about-face, walked over to the garage, and yanked the bulky door overhead with enough force to make it recoil on its springs and come crashing violently back at him.

McNabb threw two palms up, caught the door, and pushed it back in place. "Go ahead," he shrugged. "Look all you want."

The Chevrolet had been backed into the garage. I glanced at the vanity tag that said "CUDA" on the front bumper, and placed my hand on the hood. "Your engine is warm. Been someplace recently?"

"Not in *this*," McNabb said. "I haven't driven it since this afternoon. I was in Roscoe's car tonight."

I opened the driver's door and shined my flashlight on the floor and the seats hoping to find a spent casing from Roscoe's gun. No such luck.

"Where did you go when you were in Roscoe's car tonight?" I asked, turning toward him.

"Spotlighting deer."

"See any?"

"Nope!"

"So what you're saying, then, is that Junior is lying and you're telling me the truth. Right?"

"That's right."

"Why would Junior want to lie about any of this?"

McNabb shrugged. "Dunno," he said.

"Are you two enemies?"

"No."

"What then?"

29

Another shrug. His eyes, like two dead pools, showed neither fear nor concern, which led me to believe that he and Roscoe Coon had contrived a story and that nothing short of truth serum would extract a declaration of guilt from him.

But in spite of that, whenever I confront a suspect who is willing to talk I consider myself fortunate, for even when everything they say is laced with lies I'll often pick up something of value if the conversation lasts long enough.

"So," I pressed, "did you and Roscoe do anything besides spotlighting tonight?"

McNabb nodded his head emphatically and began what sounded like a rehearsed monologue about the past several hours. He claimed that he and Roscoe became bored because they couldn't find any deer, and that Roscoe decided to stop at a convenience store in Tunkhannock at 10:00 P.M. (the same time they were seen at the orchard) to get something to eat. They stayed at the store for an hour or so, he claimed, talking with two store employees whom they knew well, and then went home afterwards.

Then McNabb added something that caught me completely off guard: "Travis Crowe was in the car with us," he said. "Ask him. He'll back us up."

Now it was three against two — their favor. Apparently, two eyewitnesses for the game warden meant that they had to produce one more "witness" for their side. Unsettling, to say the least, considering their young ages.

I reckoned the two poachers had started formulating an alibi almost immediately after losing Junior and Lew on the back road, and that they decided to switch vehicles and drive to the convenience store where they could be seen by people they knew. That they found someone willing to corroborate their story, namely, one Travis Crowe, was an accomplishment in itself — one that I'm sure they'll be proud of well into adulthood.

It was useless to question McNabb any further because in his mind, he had an airtight alibi — and he could produce three witnesses to my two. I could see the conviction shining in his eyes. He had beaten me before I even showed up that night.

I terminated the interview and started back to Junior Child's house to drop him off. Along the way my deputy called by radio. I wasn't surprised to learn that he'd been handed the same story from Roscoe Coon that I got from McNabb. It was too late to do anything more that night, so I thanked Junior for his help, assuring him that the fight wasn't over yet, and started home for a few hours sleep.

The following day I paid a visit to the Tunkhannock convenience store and interviewed the two employees that McNabb had told me about. Both remembered seeing McNabb and Coon walk into the store sometime around 10:00 P.M. but couldn't be sure about the exact time. However, their shift change was at 11:00 P.M., and they were certain it was well before then.

While I had no doubts about McNabb and Coon shooting the deer, my case against them would be weakened considerably if the two store employees and Travis Crowe showed up in court to testify in their behalf. McNabb and Coon may have been young, but they were proving to be as shrewd and devious as any poacher I had come across before, and I wondered if Junior and Lew would be strong enough to stand up against them at a trial.

But later that night my outlook began to brighten when I received an unexpected phone call from a young man who said he'd been in the car with McNabb and Coon when they shot the deer.

The news left me speechless at first. "Was a man named Travis Crowe in the car with the three of you?" I asked.

"No, sir," he breathed, "but we were at Travis' house that night — Cuda, Roscoe, and me. Cuda told Travis that he was in big trouble. Asked him to say that he'd been riding around with him and Roscoe all night. That they never shot any deer. Travis said he would, too. He's scared of Cuda. Everybody is! You don't want to be around Cuda when he gets mad. He's like a crazy man." —

"Whoa," I broke in. "Take it easy; Cuda isn't going to hurt anybody. I'll see to that. Now calm down and tell me your name."

"Name's Chance. Sorry, sir. Guess I'm a little worried — and a little scared too."

"Nothing to be afraid of, son. You're doing the right thing." I hoped he believed me, and wished that we were talking face-to-face rather than on the phone. I could hear the panic in his voice, and feared he would hang up any second and blow my opportunity to crack the case wide open.

There was a long, dead silence on the other end.

"Chance? Are you still there?" I waited in agony for that inevitable *click!* followed by the low, droning hum of a line gone dead. "Hello . . . ?"

"Yeah. I'm still here."

"Look . . . you wouldn't have called if you didn't want to talk, right?"

"Yes, sir."

"Well . . ."

"But I don't want to go to jail!"

"I'll do everything in my power to see that you don't," I said. "You have my word."

Chance fell into a brief period of silence once again. I waited for what seemed an eternity before he spoke: "My brother told me you are a fair man. Stern, but fair."

"Your brother is right. Now, what else did Cuda have to say?"

"Cuda thinks Junior saw me in the car that night — that's why they want Travis to say that *he* was in the car. Cuda wants me to swear in court that I wasn't with them, too. Said he'd kick my butt if I didn't. But there is no way I can put my hand on the Holy Bible and swear to tell the truth when I'm going to tell a lie!"

No wonder Chance was so frightened. Not only did he think I'd throw him in jail if he admitted being with McNabb and Coon, but Cuda was threatening to pound the daylights out of him if he didn't lie for him. And if he did lie, the young man feared he'd face the wrath of God! He felt boxed in and I didn't blame him.

"You're a good man, Chance," I said in an attempt to put him at ease. "Good men don't lie in court. You should be proud of yourself for taking a stand against Cuda."

"I appreciate you saying that, sir, but I don't *feel* like a good man right now. I was wrong. I was in the back seat and I handed Roscoe the gun. When I heard it go off, I wanted to puke. They were out to shoot a deer. I knew it all along too. I shouldn't have gone with them . . . but . . . when they asked me . . ."

Chance hesitated briefly and then his young voice began to crack. "Honest, I've never done anything like this before. It's just that . . . well . . . I wanted them to be my friends. Cuda was a jock in school. And Roscoe, he was the class clown. They were the coolest guys, man. They had all the girls, and everybody liked them — even the teachers! I just wanted to hang with them. *Be* like them, I guess."

His words made me feel genuine pity for him. "I hope you've changed your mind by now," I said.

"Yes, sir."

"Would you be willing to testify against McNabb and Coon in court?"

"I don't know. We all work at the mill together. It's hard. They've been talking about you on the job a lot. They're scared. I've been telling them to just admit they did it, but they won't listen."

Chance paused for a moment. "My older brother knows all about it. He says I have to do whatever you want. So, yeah," he added with a weary sigh. "If you need me to testify, I will."

"Hopefully, you won't have to," I said. "Once they find out we've talked, they might just change their tune."

"I hope so," said Chance. "I hope they come clean so we can get this over with. Besides, I don't want to take time off from my job to go to court."

But when I spoke with McNabb and Coon the following day and told them about my conversation with Chance, they refused to change their story. I tried putting more pressure on them; told them they were flirting with a felony charge of intimidating a witness (ordering Chance to give false testimony or face a beating) unless they fessed up, but it didn't matter. They denied ever seeing Chance that night and claimed they had nothing to do with killing the 10-point buck.

"Just ask Travis!" insisted McNabb. "He was with us all night — not that jerk, Chance."

McNabb's blatant defiance of any moral obligation whatsoever, continued to astound me. It became quite clear that both he and Roscoe Coon were more than willing to show up in court and simply lie through their teeth. And although my likelihood of winning the case had improved dramatically with the addition of Chance's testimony, I didn't want to embroil my civilian witnesses in a lengthy court case if it could be avoided. And, so, with that in mind, I decided to play my last card.

I had always suspected that Roscoe Coon wasn't as leathery as McNabb, and knew that he lived at home with his parents, so I decided to telephone his mother, hoping she might talk some sense into her wayward son. She listened intently as I explained everything to her. When I finished she didn't offer any excuses or arguments in her son's behalf, just said she'd speak to him when he got home from work, and that she would get back to me.

I felt relieved. Although Roscoe Coon was an adult in the eyes of the law, I reckoned his parents still wielded some leverage over him since he lived in the same house. I also figured that if Roscoe came clean, Lonnie McNabb would too. He'd have no choice.

Later that same night, my phone rang and I was surprised to hear Lonnie McNabb's voice on the other end. "Just got off the phone with Roscoe's mother," he said resignedly. "Man, is she on the warpath! Told me to call you or else Roscoe would be kicked out." He paused and I could hear him breathing calmly on the other end. At length he said, "Okay. You got us! How much is it gonna cost?"

"First, I have a question," I said. "Why would you drive up behind someone you knew, and shoot a deer right out from under their spotlight?"

McNabb snorted back at me as if I had just said something funny. "We was just messing with them, man. Besides, it was Roscoe's idea — always looking to play a joke on somebody." He let out malicious giggle. "You should've seen the look on Junior's face when Roscoe shot the deer! I gotta admit it was a sick thing to do, but at the time we both thought it was pretty funny."

Man, this guy's elevator isn't going to the top floor, I thought shaking my head. Then I said, "You two comedians probably won't get as big a laugh out of the penalty for poaching: It's $1000 plus three years loss of your hunting privileges."

There was a brief silence. Then McNabb chuckled nervously. "You're joking, right?"

"No. You and Roscoe are the jokesters. I'm the serious one."

"But that's a lot of money!"

"Yes . . . it's supposed to be a deterrent."

I heard a long, pronounced sigh on the other end. Then McNabb cleared his throat and said, "Guess you couldn't give us a break, huh?"

Now it was my turn to laugh. "You two don't deserve a break, McNabb. Breaks are for people who are capable of remorse — not sociopaths like you and Coon!"

I hung up and chuckled to myself. *Sure wish I could've been a fly on the wall when Roscoe's mother lit into him!*

Although Roscoe Coon and Lonnie McNabb had no qualms about interfering with law enforcement officers, meddling with Commonwealth witnesses, or obstructing the Pennsylvania judicial system in order to avoid prosecution, in the end, they wouldn't dare mess with Mom. And I suppose, in light of that subtlety, there may be a modicum of hope for them after all.

Thou hast bound bones and veins in me,
fastened me flesh...

— Gerard Manley Hopkins

Blood and Dishonor

NOVEMBER 19, 2001.

Twelve hours had passed since Alec Callahan killed his bear, and the night had turned pitch black. Now a lone deputy sped toward the suspected poacher's cabin. He had gone ten miles on hardtop when he suddenly turned onto a dirt road and followed it into the forest. Callahan's cabin lay a half-mile ahead, and the deputy had to slow to a crawl to avoid the potholes and jagged rocks that peeked up at him along the way. He rounded a sharp bend and the road narrowed even more. Here branches of maple and oak reached out for him like long boney arms to claw at his fenders as he crept ahead.

Finally, he came to a jeep trail carved through the woods on his left. A heavy steel cable anchored between two massive oaks guarded the entrance. Deputy Jeff Pierce shut off his engine and stepped into the cold night air, the surround so still he could hear the tinny click of his flashlight as he switched it on. He swept his beam across the neighboring trees — many posted with "No Trespassing" signs — and then cast it into the gloom before him. The trail, just wide enough for a single vehicle, quickly disappeared around a bend and continued toward Callahan's cabin deep in the woods.

Ducking under the cable, Pierce noticed a thin line of corn on the trail, the tiny yellow kernels reflecting brightly in his beam. He suspected they had leaked from the tailgate of a pickup truck entering the camp with fresh bait, and his pulse quickened at the notion that someone might be there right now. He moved forward cautiously, his eyes straining through the darkness until he came to the inky silhouette of a two-story building ahead. Callahan's cabin was a mere 50 yards away, and the deputy quickly turned out his light.

Pierce wasn't about to take chances. No one expected him, and trespassers had been known to be shot in these mountains. Choosing to announce himself before moving closer, he cupped a hand to the side of his mouth and called out: *"State game warden! Anybody here?"* —

Something moved behind him!

Pivoting quickly on his heels, Pierce drew his revolver. He heard a sudden frenzied crashing through the brush. Branches snapping like two-by-fours as a shadowy form fled through the woods.

A bear! A very large bear by the sound. And it had been lurking within mere feet of him.

The deputy winked his light where the bear had been moments before and saw the reflection of a reddish-brown substance in its flash. Apples. Hundreds of them! Smashed into a pulp and dumped by the cabin, their pungent heady scent would have been a powerful draw to bears for miles around. And as he stood over the great fermenting mass, he came to know what had happened here earlier in the day . . .

The sun had finally set on the first day of Pennsylvania's bear season, and I was headed for the state bear check station when word came over my radio about bait at the Callahan camp. I had been getting complaints about Alec Callahan for some time, so it didn't surprise me to learn that his camp might be illegally baited. But I had no idea that my investigation into the matter would drag through the courts for five long years, concluding with a Supreme Court decision on search and seizure that would affect every police officer in the entire Commonwealth.

Back in the spring of 1998, I investigated a report that Callahan's camp had been baited, and was sickened to discover two dead bear cubs lying by a 20-pound slab of commercial-grade chocolate. They had gorged themselves on its sweet, rich flavor until their stomachs and intestines were crammed full.

Unfortunately for the cubs, chocolate contains a chemical compound called theobromine, which is often fatal when ingested by animals. A single pound of chocolate is enough to kill a 40-pound dog. The cubs had eaten three times more. Unable to metabolize the chemical effectively, their systems became poisoned and they died within a few feet of the beguiling delicacy.

Suspecting the chocolate had been put there during the fall hunting season to attract bears into the area, and then left behind when the men broke camp, I questioned Alec Callahan at his home regarding the incident. He categorically denied knowing anything about the chocolate, and without more information or a witness to prove otherwise, I had no choice but to walk away.

But now things would be different. The information concerning Callahan's baited camp was fresh, not six months old like before, and I welcomed the opportunity to catch him in the act. Rather than use the open airwaves and risk being picked up by scanners, I answered the radio dispatcher by cell phone and asked for the complainant's phone number. After jotting down the information, I started pushing buttons on my cell phone. It rang twice when someone answered; the voice at the other end telling me that Alec Callahan's camp was heavily baited with corn and apples, and that he may have shot a bear near the cabin.

"Look, I don't want to be involved any further in this," the informant said uneasily. "I'm afraid of retaliation."

"No problem," I replied. "Your phone call is reason enough for me to visit Callahan's camp and look around. You won't be involved any further."

"I hope you get him," the voice came back.

"I'll do my best," I promised. "You've got my word on that."

It was dark when I pulled into the state bear check station, the long line of pickup trucks loaded with trophy bears indicating another successful season for the mountain region I patrolled. Hunters usually kill between 2500 and 3500 bears during Pennsylvania's three-day season, with the majority taken on the first day. This year would be no exception, as more than 1400 bears were brought into check stations located throughout the Commonwealth that day. More than a few bruins weighed in at over 600 pounds, with one particular bear tipping the scales at a whopping 761 pounds. Pennsylvania routinely produces the heaviest black bears in North America, and currently holds the world's record for the largest black bear ever taken legally by a hunter. Ironically, only two other black bears in the world outrank it, one of which was killed illegally in Pennsylvania back in 1987.

I eased my vehicle past the awaiting trucks that stretched bumper to bumper for a hundred yards until I reached the check station. Here a state biologist and two helpers stood outside busily processing the animals. Each bear would be placed on a large scale to be weighed while throngs of curious onlookers oohed and aahed with satisfaction and surprise. After recording the bear's sex, weight, and body measurements, a small tooth would be extracted to determine the bear's age by cutting it in half and counting the rings (a blue die is applied to bring them out), much as one would count the growth rings in a tree.

After finding a place to park, I worked my way through the crowd and stepped inside the check station. Here agency personnel were sitting at desks taking pertinent information from successful hunters. My neighboring officer, Jim Jolley, had just finished thumbing through a stack of bear kill reports and smiled amiably as I walked toward him. "I heard the dispatcher call you about Callahan's camp," he said pulling a paper from the pile on his desk and handing it to me. "Looks like Alec might have gotten himself into some trouble today."

I took the paper and examined it. The information had been obtained from Alec Callahan himself earlier that morning. It showed that he had killed a 200-pound female bear in Windham Township at 6:45 A.M. — only nine minutes after the opening hour.

I glanced up at Jolley. "We need to talk to this guy."

He nodded in agreement. "Callahan lives in my district. Want to head over there?"

"Yes," I said digging into a pocket for my cell phone. "But first I want my deputy to head over to Callahan's camp and see if anybody is still around."

An hour had passed before Deputy Pierce got back to me. "I'm at the camp standing by a big pile of mashed apples," he explained over his cell phone. "I can see the front footprint of a bear pressed into them and I found blood drops on two leaves near the bait."

"Good work, Jeff!" I was amazed that he had actually been able to detect tiny blood spatters in the black of night. "Anything else?"

"I can see an impression in the apples . . . like a bear fell into them and then got back up and ran off. I think it was shot right on top of the bait."

Pierce points to blood drops just in front of apple pomace.

"Okay, Jeff. I'm going to head over to Callahan's house in a few minutes. Put the bloody leaves in an envelope, and we'll go back to the camp tomorrow when it turns light."

"Sounds good. But I'd like to look around here a bit more before heading home."

"Okay, Jeff. Good luck. I'll see you in the morning."

I pocketed my phone and looked at Jolley. "Do you know where Alec Callahan's house is located?"

"Sure do!" he beamed. "You drive and I'll navigate."

Jolley and I made the 15 miles to Callahan's place in record time, and as I turned into his driveway, my headlights swept across a bear carcass hanging by its neck from the bucket of a commercial backhoe.

"That bear has got to be ten feet off the ground," Jolley remarked as we walked toward the house. "Guess he wants to be sure the whole world can see it."

"Bragging rights," I shrugged knocking on the front door. From inside we heard the sound of heavy footsteps approaching followed by the jiggle of a latch. Then the door opened wide and Alec Callahan stood before us with a gaping jaw of surprise. He was medium height and thickset, his fiery-orange hair cut military short, cheeks ruddy, ice blue eyes narrow and piercing.

"Pennsylvania Game Commission," I announced. "This is Officer Jolley. I'm Wasserman. We'd like to talk to you about your bear." I inched suggestively toward Callahan, and he moved back and invited us inside.

We stepped into the doorway and entered a dim hallway that spilled into a modest kitchen and living room. Callahan stood firmly before us wearing a tight scowl, arms folded across his broad chest, his expression clearly warning us not to take another step. "It's tagged and I already took it to the bear check station. What's the problem?"

"We were at your camp tonight," I said. "It's baited with apples and corn, and it looks like a bear has been shot there."

Callahan shrugged off my charge. "Not at *my* camp. I was the only one around today."

"Who put the bait out?"

"I did. It's there to feed the animals. What's wrong with that?"

"We found blood near the apples. We think it's from a bear — your bear."

Callahan pressed his lips into a tight frown. "No way," he said shaking his head vehemently. "I shot my bear away from my camp."

"Where might that be?"

Callahan looked over his shoulder toward the kitchen at the end of the hallway. The light was on, and we could hear someone cleaning dinner dishes. He turned toward us, his voice lower now. "Take the woods road past my camp about a quarter mile; you'll come to a clearing where two big oak trees stand out. Walk between them, straight ahead, and you'll see where I gutted my bear. I shot it broadside as it crossed in front of me right there in the field."

I had no idea if he was telling me the truth, but one thing I did know was that bears hunt with their noses. Their sense of smell is beyond extraordinary. The slightest breeze would have carried the pungent scent of fermenting apples to every bear passing within a half mile of the camp. "If that's where you shot your bear, you were still too close to the bait," I told him.

Callahan's thick brow wrinkled with frustration. "You're crazy! I was more than 1000 feet away from the cabin. That's plenty far enough."

"Not really. If I had apples and corn dumped out at *my* camp, I wouldn't be hunting in the same township — let alone down the road apiece like you've just admitted." I paused to let my comment sink in, then said, "Look, I can have a DNA analysis done on the blood we found at your camp. If it came from your bear, we're going to know about it one way or another. Sure you don't have anything else you want to tell me?"

Callahan regarded me for a long moment, then shoved his hands into his pockets and nodded solemnly. "Yeah," he grumbled, "I'm sure. So what happens next, a ticket or something?"

"Looks that way," I said. "But first, we're going to take your bear and hold it for evidence. Citations will come later — after the lab results come back. Right now, I need you to drop the bucket on your backhoe so we can load the bear." I half expected Callahan to refuse. Just stand there with a smug look on his face as we scratched our heads trying to figure out how to get his 200-pound bear down from its iron gallows. But he surprised me.

"C'mon," he said, motioning us out the door as he squeezed by. "Let's get this over with."

We stepped outside and followed him to the backhoe. Callahan climbed aboard the big machine with the agility of a man at ease around heavy equipment. He plopped himself behind the steering wheel and keyed the ignition switch, cranking over the engine. The powerful diesel belched out a thick cloud of black exhaust and came alive with a deep, chugging rumble. Callahan pulled a lever dropping it into gear, and the backhoe lurched forward with his bear swaying to and fro in its noose. Reaching my patrol car, he stopped his rig and slowly lowered the boom, easing the bulky carcass onto the big game carrier attached to my back bumper. Then he shut down the engine and climbed from the cab as we began lashing the beast to my carrier with a sturdy nylon rope.

"Better make sure my bear is well taken care of," he warned.

I glanced up at him and gave the rope a final hearty tug. "Your bear will be just fine," I said. But inside I thought, *It's not your bear any longer, Callahan — it belongs to the Commonwealth of Pennsylvania, and you better get yourself a darn good attorney if you think you're ever going to see it again!*

The following morning Deputy Jeff Pierce arrived at my house bright and early. As a matter of fact, the sun had just peeked over the mountains when I saw his pickup truck pulling into my driveway. We were to patrol together that day, as we often did during bear seasons, and I stepped outside to greet him as he slid from behind his steering wheel. Of medium height, burly in frame, and sporting a neatly trimmed mustache, Jeff was in full uniform, his face expressionless as he reached into his top pocket and pulled out a small manila envelope. He said nothing, but nodded a silent greeting.

"Bloody leaves?" I asked

"Yep."

I nodded approvingly and took them from him. "We confiscated Callahan's bear last night," I said. "It's in the freezer back at headquarters."

"Good."

"Yeah . . . " I smiled. "Ready to go?"

Pierce turned and began walking toward his truck. "I want you to see something first," he answered casually over his shoulder. Jeff was casual by nature. He talked in a low, single-tone-of-voice, and rarely exhibited any emotion. His perpetually subdued temperament made him a great court witness, as even the most aggressive trial lawyers couldn't manage to fluster him during his testimony. Pierce, a paramedic for many years, had seen more than his share of grisly car crashes and bloody corpses, and I often wondered if his blunt disposition was the direct outcome of bearing witness to countless tragedies over the years.

Pierce snapped on a pair of latex medical gloves as I followed him to his truck. "Found this last night," he said dropping the tailgate. He stretched into the bed and retrieved a medium-sized cardboard box. Then he pulled something from inside it and turned to face me.

Cradled within his gloved hands was the bulging severed stomach of a large animal. It had been sliced open dead center with a sharp knife; a pulpy brown stew of fermented apples and undigested corn kernels oozing from the incision. "Callahan's bear," said Pierce, wrinkling his nose. "You can even smell the spoiled apples — just like at his camp."

I couldn't help but marvel at his discovery. "Nice job!" I said. "Should help us convict Callahan, all right. Where did you find it?"

"In the woods at the end of the dirt road."

"That's where Callahan said he field dressed his bear when I questioned him last night. How in the world did you know to look there?"

Pierce offered an unassuming shrug. "I wanted to poke around a little more after I left Callahan's camp," he said, "so when I got back to my truck I followed the dirt road until it ended, and then I got out and walked into the woods. I don't know why . . . something just told me to. It just seemed right." He put the bear's stomach back in the cardboard box, pulled off his latex gloves, and tossed them in with it.

"The food inside that stomach could really clinch things for us," I said. "Especially if we can get a DNA match of the blood at the camp with the entrails at the gut pile."

Pierce lifted his tailgate and rammed it shut with both hands. "Good," he nodded confidently. "Because there's absolutely no doubt in my mind that Callahan shot his bear at the bait pile. Then either he hauled the carcass into the woods at the end of the road to gut it, or the bear ran off and died back there. But I don't believe for a minute that he shot it there."

"Makes two of us," I said. "Now, do you want to show me where you found the gut pile or stand around here talking about it all morning?"

Pierce smiled at me with a crinkled eye. "No, I'm ready," he said. "Don't forget to bring your camera."

I snapped my fingers. "Ah! It's on the kitchen table. Be right back."

As I ran to the house, I heard Pierce muttering something under his breath and decided it would be best not to ask him what it was.

The entrails, minus the stomach that Pierce had removed, were exactly where Alec Callahan had said they would be — in a clearing between two big oak trees. And I could detect the sweet, lingering odor of fermented apples emanating from them as we approached. The intestines contained undigested corn, apples, and wild berries, just like the stomach had. I also noticed a conspicuous absence of acorns and beechnuts, normally found in a bear's digestive tract at this time of year.

The bear had been shot through the heart and lungs, with both organs exhibiting considerable damage. But what we didn't see was any indication that it had been shot in the immediate area. We could find no blood trail leading to the entrails. In fact, there was no blood to be found anywhere in the vicinity, lending considerable credence to our suspicion that Callahan did not shoot his bear here.

After photographing the internal organs and the surrounding terrain, I cut off a small piece of the bear's liver for evidence, hoping for a DNA match with the blood drops Pierce had found near the bait at Callahan's camp.

From here, we drove a quarter mile back to Alec Callahan's property and parked by the heavy steel cable that guarded the entrance. After grabbing a handful of evidence bags and a 300-foot measuring reel, we started hiking up the dirt lane toward Callahan's cabin.

It was a well-built, two-story wood structure on an acre of cleared forest, strategically positioned on high ground so the occupants could see anyone — or anything — coming toward them from a long distance away.

Approaching closer we saw four bait piles in the open woods. They were in a semicircle, all within plain view of the cabin. The largest pile consisted entirely of apple pomace, while the other three were made up of corn cobs, perhaps a bushel or so each, scattered upon the ground. We inspected the pile of fermenting apples first. Here Pierce pointed to an indentation that looked like it had been made by a large animal falling sideways into the pulpy mess. Nearby, the front footprint of a bear had been pressed into the pomace. The track pointed toward the entrails less than a quarter mile away, lending confidence to our suspicion that a bear had been shot at the bait and then ran off to die back in the woods where Callahan claimed he killed it.

I raised my digital camera to snap a photograph but something in the pulp suddenly caught my eye. Although the pomace was brown in color, it also contained a generous sprinkling of red skins, so I almost missed it. Something dime-sized and pinkish lay in the fermenting brew. Curious, I snapped a close-up photograph, and then plucked it out.

Front footprint of a bear in the apple pomace at Callahan's Camp.

Flesh! It looked like flesh. And it had a single black hair sticking to it.

I raised the substance to my nose, sniffed it, and knew instantly that it was muscle tissue from a bear — for nothing else smells like a bear, but a bear. Now, with no doubt in my mind that one had been targeted here, I dropped the kernel of flesh into a small manila envelope and began photographing everything in sight: the cabin, the corn, the apples, the bear track — everything. After finishing with the pictures, I moved to establish the distance from the bait to Callahan's cabin so I could testify in court, if need be, that the apple pomace wasn't within the curtilage (the area immediately surrounding a house or dwelling) of Callahan's cabin, but rather in an open field and in plain view. Otherwise, I risked having all evidence discovered on the property thrown out for lack of a search warrant.

Standing by the apples I held the end-clip on my tapeline while Pierce reeled it back to Callahan's cabin. "Thirty-two yards!" he hollered reaching the front wall. I waved a hand of acknowledgement and raised my eyes to the second-story balcony ten feet above him. A door led to it from inside the cabin.

Corncobs were scattered in three piles at the Callahan Camp.

Pierce started back toward me, winding the tape measure into its reel as he approached. Drawing near he stopped briefly, glanced back over his shoulder, and shook his head grimly. "Callahan probably shot the bear right from the balcony," he scoffed.

"It was definitely shot from above," I said. "Jolley and I took a good look at the bear before we put it in the freezer last night. We found one bullet wound. And it entered from a high angle through the bear's back between the shoulder and spine."

Pierce bunched his lips in speculation and stared into the woods behind me. "Bear weighed around 200 pounds, didn't it?"

"Yeah . . ."

"Pretty heavy, huh?" he asked sagely.

"No handles on a bear," I chuckled. "Just dead weight."

"Thinking what I'm thinking right now?"

"That he must have had help loading it into his truck?"

"Yeeeup!"

I nodded my head solemnly. *Callahan couldn't have lifted a two hundred pound bear alone,* I thought. *Of course he had help! And it was probably his old friend, Joe Gunner.*

I had been after Gunner for years, and had finally caught up with him last winter, just after buck season ended. He'd been cruising the back roads looking for another "trophy" to add to his collection when he spotted a nice 10-pointer grazing in a sunny pasture along with several Holsteins. A house and barn stood just beyond the cows, but that wasn't enough to stop Joe Gunner from taking a crack at the deer. Little did he know, however, that he would soon come to terms with a courageous mother and her three spirited children. It was an ugly incident, and it came back to me in a sudden flash of memory:

As Gunner eased his pickup toward the unsuspecting whitetail that day, Michael and his mother happened to be watching the deer from a kitchen window, pleased that it had survived the hunting season. Neither of them saw Gunner's truck as it crept toward the deer. Their property, hemmed by a heavy growth of cedars, shielded the road from their view.

But ten-year-old Stephanie, playing inside the open barn fifty yards away, could see the road plain as day. She watched curiously as the dark truck slowed to a stop. She could even hear the sharp popping of gravel being crushed beneath its tires. And when the driver suddenly brought his vehicle to a stop and pointed a rifle out the window, she buried her tiny face in her hands.

Her 14-year-old brother, Eddie, looked up when he heard the shot. Busy with barn chores, he was shocked to see a deer thrashing on the ground and a man leaping from his pickup truck cradling a rifle. Eddie dropped his pitchfork and ran across the field as fast as his legs would carry him. He reached the truck in a matter of seconds, his chest pounding. "Are you crazy!" he screamed. "It's not even deer season!"

Joe Gunner, a lean, hawk-faced man in his mid-thirties with shoulder-length silver-blonde hair, calmly slipped back into his truck and shoved it into gear. He glared down at the boy. "Better get out of my way, kid. I got places to be."

"No, you better wait right here, mister," demanded Eddie. "My mother is gonna want to speak with you!"

All at once, Eddie saw his brother, Michael coming toward them in his Ford Mustang. Gunner spotted him too. Slamming his foot on the accelerator, he fled down the dirt road in a cloud of brown dust.

Michael skidded to a stop. Eddie hopped in beside him and they sped down the road. Within seconds, they were right behind Gunner. "There's a pen in my glove box," barked Michael. "Get it and write his license number on your hand." Eddie did as his brother directed, and Michael quickly backed off. Gunner was driving at a reckless pace, and Michael decided to return home and call a game warden rather than continue following him.

Joe Gunner ended up being cited for killing a deer in closed season, hunting from a vehicle, and hunting too close to a residence. He hired a good attorney, the case went to court, and Gunner pled not guilty in front of the judge. But it was to no avail. Michael, Eddie, Stephanie, and their mother voluntarily appeared as my witnesses at his trial, and he was convicted of all charges. Gunner's fines totaled well over $1000, in addition, his hunting license was revoked for three years.

But I doubted that Gunner's conviction had stopped him from hunting for one second — probably just made him more careful. And I also suspected he'd been at Callahan's camp yesterday and helped him with his bear. But if he had, it was highly unlikely that Callahan would ever admit it. Alec Callahan might have been a lot of things, but he wasn't a rat.

Returning my thoughts to the task at hand, I regarded the photographs and blood evidence we had collected, and, confident we had enough to prosecute Callahan, decided to head back to my patrol car. Bear season was in its second day; Pierce and I still had 400 square miles of mountainous terrain to cover.

After storing our evidence and other gear in my vehicle, we began driving out the narrow woods road, away from Callahan's camp, when a white van suddenly came at us from out of nowhere. The driver certainly must have realized that a law enforcement vehicle blocked his path. A red emergency lightbar spanned the roof of my patrol car. You couldn't miss it. Yet the van continued to rocket straight at us while the road, hemmed in by mature trees, made it impossible to maneuver out of the way.

I slammed my brakes. "Take cover, now!"

As Pierce and I bailed out, we saw the van sliding to a jittery stop and I wondered if some madman was about to leap from the vehicle with an AK-47 in his hands, a twisted smile frozen on his lunatic face as he emptied a magazine full of hot lead at us.

At the time, the entire country was on the lookout for two men in a white van that had been on a killing-spree in several neighboring states. Thirteen innocent people had been randomly shot, with ten killed and three badly injured during the past three weeks. The victims were mostly men, but several women were also killed. Even a 13-year-old boy had been shot and critically injured after exiting a school bus. Known as The Beltway Sniper, news of his latest victims had been blaring across TV screens, radio stations, and the front page of newspapers far and wide for days on end. What made the incidents exceptionally startling was that people were being picked off in broad daylight as they mowed lawns, walked through mall parking lots, or pumped gasoline into their tanks at busy service stations.

With that grim thought in mind, I stationed myself alongside Pierce behind my Chevy Blazer. We both drew our .357 magnum revolvers while the morning sun glared against the van's windshield, its harsh reflection making it impossible to see anyone inside as the vehicle came to a jarring halt inches from my front bumper.

"STATE GAME COMMISSION! GET OUT WITH YOUR HANDS UP!" I roared.

We waited as the van crouched in front of us like some giant brooding beast, my ears straining to detect any movement — the creak of a back door inching open, a side window squeaking down — anything that might warn of an attack. But there was only silence, save the steady rhythmic tick of the van's cooling engine. Then, after what seemed an eternity, the driver's door began to ease open. We kept our guns trained at the figure stepping to the ground: Medium height and stocky, hands raised high over his head, shock and disbelief written on his face —

Alec Callahan.

Idiot! I thought, shaking my head in disbelief. Stepping from behind my vehicle I stood with my gun pointed toward him. "Keep your hands in the air," I warned.

Jeff instinctively went forward and frisked Callahan for weapons while I covered him. His hands worked their way over his clothing, searching for a hidden gun, while Callahan eyed me with open contempt. Finished, Pierce turned my way. "He's clean."

I holstered my revolver. Callahan spat hard on the ground. "I can't believe you had your gun pointed at me!" he snapped, his ruddy cheeks turning bright crimson.

His self-important arrogance was no less than astounding. I could feel my hackles start to rise. "What did you expect, pulling a stupid stunt like that?"

Callahan's jaw fell slack for a moment, as if no one had ever accused him of being stupid before. I watched his brow wrinkle with resentment and waited for him to make another dumb remark. Almost begged him to.

Pierce rolled his eyes and stepped in quickly. "Sir," he said, placing a hand on Callahan's shoulder, "how 'bout we go over to our patrol car and get you inside. It's freezing out here and we'd like to talk to you further about your bear."

Callahan shrugged off the deputy's hand and glared at me. "Is that what *you* want?"

Thankful that Pierce had intervened, I exhaled slowly, gradually transforming my face into one of genuine compassion. "I'd like to hear anything you're willing to tell me," I said. Then, with a half-nod at my Blazer, "Why don't we step into my office."

Pierce remained outside while I slipped into my vehicle with Alec Callahan. A sharp, cold wind had picked up and I was glad to be away from it. Deputy Pierce, on the other hand, knew better than to seek a comfortable back seat to my forthcoming "chat" with Callahan. I had done hundreds of interviews and interrogations over the years, and prided myself on the number of confessions I'd been able to attain. Pierce knew I preferred to question suspects on a one-on-one basis. It's easier to get someone to talk freely when they don't feel overwhelmed by interrogators. And, so, Pierce obediently stood outside with his back to my vehicle. But my deputy possessed the uncanny ability to hear sounds at distances far greater than anyone I'd ever met, and I knew he'd be able to make out every word that would be spoken between us.

Callahan was still fuming. He stared out the windshield with a scowl on his face, arms folded tightly. "I can't believe you had a gun pointed at me!"

"We are police officers, Mr. Callahan," I began. "My vehicle is a marked patrol car. You had to know that. When someone comes barreling straight at us like you did, we have no choice but to assume that they intend to do us harm. We simply responded the way that any trained law enforcement officer would have."

Callahan adjusted his weight, squinted at me sourly, and ran a thick hand through his red hair. "Didn't intend to hurt nobody. I saw your patrol car and got mad. That's all."

I shrugged it off and turned to the more important matter at hand. "I'd like to ask you some questions, Mr. Callahan, but first I want to advise you of your rights."

"Why? Am I under arrest?"

"Absolutely not. You're free to open the door and walk away any time you wish. Still want to talk?"

"I'm here aren't I?"

I pulled a plastic card from my coat pocket and began reading aloud what's commonly known as the Miranda warning. It stems from a 1966 Supreme Court decision, *Miranda v Arizona*, mandating that someone under arrest must be informed of his or her right to remain silent and to have legal counsel prior to being asked any incriminating questions. Now, Alec Callahan wasn't under arrest. In fact, I had just told him he was free to leave. But we did have our guns pointed at him earlier, and he was sitting in a law enforcement vehicle with a uniformed officer who was about to ask incriminating questions that would most definitely be used against him. And I knew that if the case went to court, a defense attorney might argue that two armed police officers had bullied his defenseless client into a confession by scaring him half to death with their "loaded guns," and then locking him inside a police vehicle without advising him of his rights. I didn't want that.

When I finished reading the Miranda warning, I asked Callahan if he understood his rights, and if he was still willing to talk to me without an attorney present. Callahan laced his fingers across this belly, pursed his lips, and nodded pensively. "Ask away!" he said.

I began by informing Callahan that I had found additional blood evidence near the apples at his camp this morning, and that it was looking more and more like he'd killed his bear at the bait pile.

"Not me!" he protested. "I told you before . . . I killed my bear at the end of the road."

"But you knew your camp was baited . . . "

"Yeah. So what? I wanted to feed the animals."

I decided to play along. "Gotcha. So you're at the end of the road, and . . ."

"I left camp and walked to the end of the dirt road, first thing in the morning. Soon as I got there, I saw a bear come out of the woods in front of me — *BOOM!* Dead bear."

Nodding in mock appreciation I asked, "How far away was the bear?"

"Maybe 50 yards or so."

"What direction was it traveling?"

"It came out of the trees to my right and crossed in front of me."

"So you shot it broadside?"

"Yeah."

"Then what?"

"The bear dropped right where I shot it and I walked over and gutted it."

"Mind showing me the gut pile?"

"I'll take you there right now if you want."

I started my engine and signaled Pierce to climb in the back seat. "Cold out?" I grinned as he squeezed in behind us.

"Nah!" He said with a straight face. Pierce looked frozen stiff but would never have admitted it. "Where we going?" he asked innocently.

I glanced at him through my rearview mirror. "Mr. Callahan is going to show us his gut pile."

Pierce nodded back; his discreet smile telling me he already knew, and that he had heard everything.

It was imperative for our suspect to physically take us to the gut pile we had found and admit that it belonged to his bear, because if the case went to trial, we needed to show the court that the entrails were indeed from Callahan's kill, by his own admission, and that they could not have come from another bear shot by someone else.

We drove back to the end of the dirt road and followed Callahan on foot until he led us to the gut pile we had discovered earlier. "This is it!" he said pointing to the guts. "That's my bear."

"You're saying that these entrails came from the bear you shot yesterday?" I asked.

"That's right."

"The same bear I took from your property last night?"

"Yeah."

"And this is where the bear dropped when you shot it?"

"Yep."

"Hmmm . . ."

Callahan cocked his head and looked at me with a narrow eye. "What's *that* mean?"

"Amazing, really," I replied with a half-shrug. "You take a short stroll down a country lane on the first day of bear season, a bear conveniently walks right out in front of you minutes after the opening hour, and you drop it in its tracks at 50-yards with one well-placed shot. Not bad!"

Callahan smiled, his teeth blinding white.

"Only one problem," I added.

"What's that?"

"I don't believe you. I think the only hunting you did yesterday was from the balcony of your cabin. And after I send the tissue and blood samples we collected to the US Fish & Wildlife Lab for a DNA analysis, I think I'll be able to put your bear right on top of the apples where you shot it."

"Whoa!" Callahan's smile quickly faded into a deep frown of concern. "Let's talk about this a bit more."

"I'm listening."

He shifted his eyes toward Deputy Pierce and back to me. "In private."

I nodded in agreement and escorted him back to my Blazer where Callahan and I sat comfortably inside while Pierce stood in the cold with his back to us once again.

Alec Callahan turned his upper body toward me. "I gotta confide something," he said soberly.

"Okay . . ."

"When you and the other warden showed up last night and took my bear — " He paused for a moment, swallowed hard, and stared out his window at my deputy. "He can't hear me, can he?"

"He'd have to be Superman to hear you right now, don't you think?"

Callahan nodded stiffly. "Yeah."

"What was it you wanted to tell me?"

"First, how much is the fine?"

"It's $800 for the bear and $200 for hunting over bait," I said. "That comes to $1000 plus another $35 for court costs."

"Look," Callahan said nervously, "when you took my bear last night I had some guests over for dinner. It was embarrassing. I don't want them or anyone else to know about this. I'd like to keep it between the two of us. Is there some way you can help me out?"

"The fines are set by law," I said. "They can't be reduced. But what I *can* do is write two citations here and now. On the back of each one, there's a section where you can plead guilty. Then you can walk into the district judge's office, hand the paperwork to her secretary, and pay your fine right there. No one has to know anything but you and me."

Callahan looked up at me. "That's it?"

I was momentarily stunned. What did he expect me to do, send him packing with a warning never to do it again? Bear poaching is considered a major wildlife crime.

I stared back at him. "Ah, Yeah . . ."

Callahan folded his arms across his broad chest and pushed his lips into a deep frown of discontent. "I guess I'll have to think about it."

Then it hit me like a freight train: Maybe Callahan wasn't asking for a break. Maybe he wanted me to hold out my palm and see how much it would be worth if I forgot about the whole thing.

Is there some way you can help me out? —

I decided not to push it any further. It would be useless to accuse him. If I were wrong, he'd be highly offended — and rightly so. If right, he would simply deny it. Say I was nuts. I turned toward him, my eyes boring into his. "I guess we don't have anything to discuss after all."

Callahan nodded reflectively. "Yeah," he muttered. "I guess you're right."

The conversation was over. I dropped Alec Callahan off at his van, had him move it out of my way, and left him.

As Deputy Pierce and I began our routine patrol for the day, Pierce remained silent, his keen eyes diligently scanning the woods as we made our way through the rugged mountains of Wyoming County. Hunting pressure was light, and soon Pierce turned to stare at me in long, contemplative silence.

I glanced at him with a questioning brow. "What?"

"Superman . . . ?"

I offered a brief half-smile and kept my eyes in front of me. "Couldn't think of anything else to say. You did hear us, didn't you?"

"Yep."

I shook my head with wonder.

"What do you think Callahan meant when he asked you to help him out?" asked Pierce.

"I don't know, but the more I think about it the more I don't like it."

"He should've taken the citations and just plead guilty. It would save everyone a lot of time and energy."

"Money too," I added. "Lawyers don't come cheap. But I don't think he intends to do that. So, tomorrow, I'm going to take a tissue sample from Callahan's bear and send it to the Fish and Wildlife Lab along with everything else we have. I want to do a bullet trajectory analysis too. Need to show that it was shot from above."

"Want me to be there?"

"No. I want you out on patrol. You're familiar with Callahan's camp, and I might need you to go back in. I'll ask Deputy Gaydos to assist me."

Frozen rock solid, its legs splayed awkwardly in four different directions, Alec Callahan's bear lay flattened atop a jumble of confiscated deer, bobcats, otters, and other carcasses tagged for evidence and stored inside the Game Commission's walk-in freezer.

"Looks like we're not the only ones catching poachers," remarked Gaydos.

"Job security," I said dryly. "How 'bout you grab the back end and I take the front. With any luck we'll get this thing out of here without rupturing ourselves."

Gaydos and I lifted the steel-like carcass and slowly wrestled it outside, stumbling clumsily over the tangle of frozen animal bodies as we went.

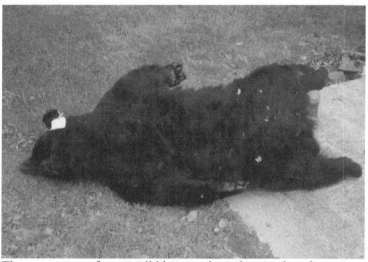

The carcass was frozen solid in an awkward, spread-eagle manner.

Finally, after all but falling out of the storage freezer, we staggered back outside, dropped Callahan's bear on the ground, and began wheezing like two chain-smokers in a jumping jack competition. "Man, we need a bigger freezer!" I coughed.

"That or fewer outlaws," puffed Gaydos.

I chuckled at the notion as I pulled a heavy-bladed knife from my belt and hacked a half-dollar-sized chunk of meat from the bear's open abdominal cavity. Taking a plastic evidence bag from my coat pocket, I dropped the frozen meat inside, and then started looking around for something we could use to prop up the bear —

"Up to no good, as usual!" boomed a voice from behind.

I whipped my head around to see Ron Eovitch leaning against the tailgate of my patrol vehicle, his long arms folded comfortably across his chest. Eovitch stood an imposing six foot four, and was in charge of maintenance for the agency.

"Hey Ron!" I called. "Where've you been hiding? I need some help."

"Known that for years, Bill. Glad you finally came to grips with yourself!"

"Very funny," I grumbled with a feigned sneer.

Gaydos snorted out loud while Eovitch managed to cling to his sober stare, hoping I'd crack before he did. But I saw his chin start to quiver and then his face broke into an enormous smile, which got all three of us giggling like a bunch of dopey schoolboys. After we settled down, Eovitch pushed himself off my tailgate and we shook hands. "Good one!" I smiled.

"You're an easy target."

"So I've heard! How have you been, anyway?"

"Good, real good. What do you need help with?"

"A bullet trajectory analysis. Do you still have any of those steel rods that we use for staking beaver traps back in your shop?"

"Sure do. Gonna run one through him?"

"That's the plan."

"Then you'll need some heat too," declared Eovitch. "And I don't see a propane torch hanging on that gun belt you're wearing."

"Left home without it again!" I quipped.

Eovitch smiled sarcastically. "I'll let you use mine, but you're gonna owe me, Bill."

"Coffee and donuts on me," I smiled. "Now, how about something we can use to raise the bear a couple feet off the ground?"

Eovitch wrinkled his brow. "What do you want to do that for?"

"The carcass is frozen flat as a mackerel," I explained. "We need to reproduce the bear's height to the same level it was when shot standing on all fours."

Eovitch thought for a moment, then turned and motioned us with a wave of his hand. "I know just what you need," he beckoned. "C'mon with me."

Gaydos and I trailed Eovitch to the rear of an adjacent storage building where we saw a huge stack of wooden cargo pallets. Pulling two from the pile, we carried them back to Callahan's bear and laid them on the ground, one atop the other. Then all three of us lifted the stiff-as-a-board carcass onto the makeshift platform, and I stepped back to admire our work.

"Perfect!" I announced cheerily.

"I don't know about perfect, but it'll do," said Eovitch. "I'll go get my torch and a length of rebar." And with that, he hustled back to his shop and disappeared through the doorway.

Waiting for Eovitch to return, Deputy Gaydos and I took advantage of the daylight and combed through every inch of the bear's dense fur searching for any wounds that Jim Jolley and I may have missed with our flashlights the night we confiscated the beast. But there was only the single dime-sized bullet hole in the back of its right shoulder that we had discovered previously. I worked my fingers into the heavy pelt, pushing back on the fur around the wound to see what direction the bullet had come from, and discovered a faint inch-long groove in the bear's skin that led directly into the bullet hole. Made by a skidding bullet, the gash pointed back toward the bear's head like an accusing finger. There could be no mistake, the shooter had been in front of the beast shooting down at it from a high angle, not standing broadside on level ground as Callahan had claimed.

Rolling the heavy carcass on its back, we peered into the open chest cavity and saw that the slug had traveled through it at a 45-degree angle and exited by shattering two ribs. (I pictured the shaggy beast with its head down, gorging on apples as Callahan stood on his balcony and squinted into his scope.) And that was all well and good, but I needed to demonstrate my findings clearly enough so that a judge could perceive how the bear was killed. In order to do that, he would have to see what we were seeing; hence, it was imperative that I illustrate the bullet's path as best I could. After all, there was a chance that the blood evidence we found at Callahan's baited camp would not match up with his bear — it could have been from some other bear that had been shot there. And the possibility loomed, albeit slight, that the evidence would be lost or destroyed after I submitted it. The United States Fish and Wildlife Forensics Lab — the only facility in the world dedicated to solving wildlife crimes — was thousands of miles away, in Oregon. What if the evidence never got there? What if they misfiled it or accidentally disposed of it? The Lab was handling more than 900 cases annually — it could happen.

Without the blood evidence, my entire case would come down to the bullet trajectory analysis alone. I had to show that the bear had been shot from above — from the balcony at Callahan's cabin — and that it could not have been shot broadside on the relatively flat terrain near the gut pile where Callahan claimed he killed it.

But when Ron Eovitch strolled toward us with a huge smile of confidence pasted on his face, I had a hunch that everything would be just fine. For in his arms was a forty-pound propane gas tank complete with hose and burner, a 4-foot section of 3/8-inch steel reinforcement rod, and a matching length of blazing white PVC pipe.

I looked at Gaydos and smiled. "Nice!" I said in a low voice. "He even brought something to slide over the steel rod so it'll stand out in a photograph."

"Great idea," said Gaydos. "Gonna tell him?"

"Nah."

Deputy Gaydos with mock rifle illustrating bullet trajectory.

Gaydos and Ron Eovitch (on ladder) demonstrate bullet path.

Eovitch set the steel gas tank by the carcass, stooped on one knee, and turned open the control valve. A steady hiss streamed from the brass burner's tapered end as he grabbed a steel spark-lighter from his back pocket. Holding the lighter directly in front of the torch, he repeatedly squeezed its spring-like handle until there was a sudden sharp pop followed by a pencil-thin blue and orange flame shooting from the burner tip. Eovitch rolled his flame over the last few inches of rod until he saw a generous plume of white smoke begin to rise from the metal. Then he handed the rod to me, and with gloved hands I carefully inserted it into the bullet hole, the hot metal crackling like bacon as I eased it into the passageway created by the slug that had torpedoed through Callahan's bear. It was slow going, and I had to pull the rod out to reheat it several times, but I kept at it, eventually managing to work it all the way through the wound. The rod had been four feet long, and the remaining three feet jutted from the bear's furry carcass like the shaft of a warrior's spear. I grabbed the white PVC pipe that Eovitch had brought, slid it over the protruding rod, and stepped back to admire my work.

Eovitch stood next to me and put his hands on his hips. "Looks like the bear was shot from a tree stand!"

I glanced at him and smiled. "Something like that."

The legwork was over. I had taken the investigation as far as I could without scientific evidence to back up my theory that Callahan had shot his bear at the bait near his cabin. Now the paperwork would begin. It was crucial that I have all my ducks in a row, as the district judge in whose court I'd be filing the charges would often tell me. And I was about to make certain her advice would be adhered to. After all, it had served me well in the past. I hadn't lost a case in her court for 17 years, and I wasn't about to let this be the first one.

Unfortunately, I can't say the same for every judge I dealt with over my long career. Although most were fair and honorable, some were wishy-washy at best, making it extremely difficult to win a case due to their apathy toward the Commonwealth's wildlife laws. The fact that most wildlife violations in Pennsylvania were classified as summary offenses, rather than more serious misdemeanors, didn't help much either. Some judges complained that our fines were excessive, and, feeling sorry for the defendants, would dismiss the charges against them so they wouldn't have to pay. Others were easily swayed by phone calls from local politicians or intimidated by high-priced defense attorneys. One district judge I dealt with was so inhospitable that I refused to patrol in his magisterial district unless I received a complaint about a violation in progress.

And then there was the district judge who once confessed to me that he grew up being taught to hate game wardens. I had known him for years prior to his appointment as a judge, and was surprised to learn this. Fortunately, I managed to build a good reputation with him, and he soon realized that we played a vital role in wildlife conservation, not only for hunters, but for all people who loved nature. As a result, his negative attitude eventually changed to one of respect and appreciation.

But District Judge Patricia Robinson never let politicians influence her decisions, nor was she intimidated by arrogant, loudmouthed defense attorneys. She also didn't put up with sloppy courtroom procedure by the prosecuting officer. If you had all your ducks in a row, and you proved your case beyond a reasonable doubt, you won.

If not, you lost. Simple as that.

With the above in mind, I gathered together all the physical evidence that I had collected from Callahan's bear, and prepared it for the evidence lab by packaging the contents in three separate envelopes and stapling a yellow evidence tag to each one. The yellow tags were an integral component of the chain of possession that every law enforcement officer must follow when handing evidence over to another agency. Each tag was individually numbered and contained a range of information about the case, including the suspect's name, date and time of the alleged violation, and a description of the contents. After placing the articles into a refrigerated shipping box, I enclosed an Evidence Submittal Form listing my instructions as follows:

Item Description:

Item #1: Manila envelope containing blood, tissue, and hair taken from suspect's camp.
Item #2: Plastic envelope containing tissue and hair from suspect's black bear taken from his residence.
Item #3: Manila envelope containing internal organ material from suspect's black bear found along woods road.

Special Examination Instructions:

Determine if item #1 is from a black bear.
Determine if item #1 DNA matches item #2 DNA.
Determine if item #3 is from a black bear.
Determine if item #3 DNA matches item #2.

This was crucial to my case, for without scientific forensic evidence, I couldn't prove that the spatters on the leaves at Callahan's camp were anything more than cherry flavored Kool-Aid. What's more, I had to show that the spatters were blood from a bear — preferably, Callahan's bear — otherwise, all Callahan had to do was say he cut himself peeling apples and that it was *his* blood on the leaves.

If everything turned out the way I expected, when the results came back I'd be able to show the court that the DNA from the blood and muscle tissue discovered at Callahan's camp matched the DNA from the gut pile discovered in the woods as well as the bear we had seized at Callahan's house.

But I also took comfort in the fact that I had an ace in the hole if the evidence happened to be lost in transit or destroyed — or even suppressed by the court for some reason: Callahan's claim that he killed his bear 1600 feet from the bait could go a long way toward a guilty conviction.

In recent years prior, I had won two similar (but distinctly separate) cases before Judge Robinson. Both were appealed all the way to the Commonwealth Court of Pennsylvania, where they were affirmed by a panel of three judges. In light of these model cases, I believed it might be possible to convict Alec Callahan based solely upon his admission that he knowingly placed bait at his camp and then killed a bear on the first day of the season a mere quarter mile away.

But I didn't want to win it that way because I didn't believe that was how it went down. Not for one second. I believed Alec Callahan ambushed his bear by shooting it in the back right from the balcony of his comfy cabin as the unsuspecting bruin slobbered over the bait he had left for it. And hoping to prove just that, I forwarded my evidence via UPS Air, next day service, to the United States Fish & Wildlife Forensics Laboratory in Ashland, Oregon.

After waiting the better part of a year for the results to come back, I finally received a reply in the mail. It arrived via Federal Express in a large blue envelope marked United States Department of the Interior — Fish and Wildlife Service. After taking a deep breath, I opened the envelope and found a two-page document inside titled GENETICS EXAMINATION REPORT. My eyes danced down the first page searching for the final results, but there was only a bunch of preliminary information about how the examination had been conducted at the lab. I quickly flipped to the second page, dropping to the final paragraph. It said **CONCLUSION:** *LAB-1, LAB-2, and LAB-3 originated from the same individual North American Black Bear.*

It had been worth the wait. We had a match!

Now certain that I had enough evidence to convict Alec Callahan in a court of law, I filed two criminal charges against him: one for unlawfully taking wildlife, and the other for hunting illegally through the use of bait. Combined they carried a total $1000 penalty.

Callahan responded by hiring a well-known defense attorney named Angelo Belli to represent him in court. Belli was a former county prosecutor with a reputation for being a tenacious fighter. And since he had experience at both ends of the spectrum, I expected a real battle.

He didn't disappoint me.

NOVEMBER 20, 2002.

The first of four ensuing court battles against Alec Callahan came before District Justice Patricia A. Robinson in Tunkhannock, Pennsylvania.

Several months prior to the trial, I had mulled over the idea of just how to present my DNA evidence in court. Flying a forensic specialist into Pennsylvania from Oregon to testify would be costly. Somebody would have to pay for it, and it wasn't going to be me. Personally, I thought a certified copy of the lab results should suffice, so I had telephoned Angelo Belli and asked if he would stipulate to the DNA evidence if I produced certified documentation from the U.S. Fish and Wildlife Forensics Laboratory. After all, I reasoned, why fly a forensic specialist across the country to testify about something we could all read on a piece of paper — besides, I intended to have the judge order his client to pay for the airfare if he was found guilty. It could save Callahan a bundle of money.

Belli didn't go for it.

And so it was 9:00 A M. as I sat in the small rural courtroom with forensics specialist Jim LeMay and wardens Jeff Pierce, Jim Jolley, and Gene Gaydos when I heard the creak of a door behind me, and turned to see Angelo Belli stroll confidently into the room escorting a female stenographer.

Mid-forties, well tanned, and of medium height and athletic build, he wore a black, three-button Armani suit and handmade wingtip shoes. His thick, raven hair was combed back tight and fell into a conspicuous shoulder-length ponytail. We were here for a trial on a wildlife violation considered a summary offense in Pennsylvania (Defendants sustain no criminal record if convicted of summary offenses.). I could count on one hand the number of times I saw a lawyer show up with a stenographer for a summary hearing. Stenographers don't come cheap. They record every spoken word in a trial by shorthand. Lawyers use them for one reason: to trap you in a misstatement when the case is appealed to a higher court.

Not that Belli expected to lose. Oh no. In fact, I'm sure the high-priced attorney thought he'd make a bumbling fool out of me in virtually no time. After all, we were in Hillbilly Junction, USA — and I was just some lowly game warden he'd have for breakfast this morning. But he wanted to make sure he covered all the bases. Angelo Belli was a good attorney. A very good attorney indeed. He rarely made mistakes and he never took risks. And although the odds were slim at best, there was always the chance that his client would be convicted. The stenographer was Belli's ace in the hole. It would give him a second chance to mess with my brain if Alec Callahan was found guilty and we met again in a higher court.

But what Angelo Belli didn't know was that I hated to lose. It was more than an ego thing with me — although that certainly accounted for some of it — winning was important because word travels in rural America. And it travels fast. If the bad guy beats you in court, he brags to his friends. And they tell all their friends. And then you start to look weak. And if it happens often enough the bad guys stop fearing you. They get bold. And they start killing with impunity because they become convinced that they can get away with it. I couldn't let that happen. The guardianship of wildlife in Wyoming County was my responsibility, and I couldn't let that happen.

I had dealt with plenty of criminal defense lawyers over the years. Some were decent and ethical professionals; others were just thugs with briefcases who loved to browbeat you in court. Intimidation, bewilderment, and confusion were their weapons. They could hurt you, ruin you, even kill you. But they did it without leaving a mark on your body. It was your reputation they wanted. Your integrity. And in the lawman's universe, that was everything. They used words instead of their fists. And if you let them get inside your head they would hammer away at you like a merciless prizefighter, leaving you bruised and stammering on the witness stand. And then you'd watch your case fall apart — everything you worked for, finished. And it would be like a fist in the gut.

Oh, you could beat them at their game all right. You could beat the very best of them. But you had to be prepared. Wars are best won through planning and knowledge and strategy. In this way, the battle is over even before the fighting begins. You had to know where your case was weak. You had to *become* your enemy. You looked at your evidence and your witnesses and your testimony, and you thought about how your opponent would attack each of them. Then you strengthened these weak areas so he couldn't get inside you.

Besides, you had the one thing a criminal defense attorney could never have: You had the truth. And if you didn't, you had no right being there. Truth is reality. It can't be altered. But most importantly, truth cannot be defeated. Unless, of course, you allow it to.

And that is why I had spent almost every hour of every working day in the last two weeks interviewing my witnesses and reviewing legal documents in preparation for Angelo Belli's grand entrance into Judge Robinson's courtroom. Did I have a few butterflies flitting around inside my guts? Yeah. After all, Belli had spent years studying law in college, and then went on to become a disciplined attorney with a stellar reputation. He worked for a big law firm, wrote legal briefs for a living, and knew every trick in the book when it came to winning a case in court. And although I had considerable courtroom experience, it was miniscule at best compared to the day in and day out affiliation with legal procedures that most attorneys cultivate over the years.

So I was a bit surprised when Belli walked over and asked if he could talk to me in private before the hearing commenced. I knew there was only one reason he would do this: he wanted to play Let's Make a Deal. But I wasn't interested. My team was sitting behind me in steel-backed chairs, prepped and ready to go. LeMay had traveled almost 3000 miles to be here, and I knew his testimony would prove devastating to the defense. What's more, I had spent weeks building a solid case against Alec Callahan. A plea deal would be out of the question. But, to be civil, I got up from my seat and accompanied the attorney into an adjacent conference room where we could talk in private.

Angelo Belli closed the door behind us, switched on the florescent lights, and set his leather briefcase on a wooden table that stood in the center of the room. "Have a seat," he offered taking a chair for himself.

I pulled a chair from the table, sat down, and waited for him to speak. Belli folded a leg over his knee and eyed me with a smooth, predatory grin. "I want to give you the opportunity to walk away from this," he said in a voice that sounded like a father offering advice to a wayward son. And I have to admit, he had me for a moment. I expected him to play the intimidation game at some point in the trial, but didn't think it would happen this soon.

"Walk away? Why would I want to do that?"

"Because you overextended your authority when you entered my client's property without a search warrant."

"No, I didn't."

"Officer Wasserman, surely you're familiar with the most rudimentary rules of criminal procedure — probable cause, constitutional rights, that sort of thing . . ."

"Very familiar."

"Then surely you must realize that you violated my client's constitutional rights when you entered his property to search for evidence of a crime without first obtaining a search warrant."

I kept silent, knowing that if he had reviewed the state game laws thoroughly he wouldn't have been so sure of himself.

"But we're willing to overlook that glaring fact," he added, "— willing to let you walk away from forthcoming consequences . . . provided you withdraw the charges against my client."

Nice try, I thought. "Forthcoming consequences" was lawyer jargon for, "I'm gonna sue your butt off if you don't do what I say." The idea of being sued for violating Callahan's constitutional rights didn't appeal to me one bit. But I had been threatened with lawsuits in the past and always shrugged it off as a hazard of the job that all lawmen face from time to time. Still, I didn't like being threatened. I stood and pushed my chair into the table. The attorney did likewise. "We should get back to the courtroom," I said. "The judge doesn't like to be kept waiting."

Angelo Belli shook his head disapprovingly, took his briefcase from the table, and politely excused himself as he brushed hurriedly by. He wanted to be first to walk back into court. Psychologically, it would imply his commanding presence to everyone in the room, especially his client. And I was okay with that. But now the showboating was over. It was time to lay all our cards on the table.

The courtroom wasn't much bigger than the average two-car garage, with the judge's ample wooden desk situated at the far wall as we entered. Belli sat with his client behind a writing table that faced the judge's desk on the left side of the room, while I took my seat at an identical table to the right. Behind me were several rows of folding chairs for any spectators who might be present. Today they were empty save my four witnesses.

All heads turned when Judge Patricia Robinson walked into the room through a doorway to our left. Belli and I rose from our chairs in mutual respect. In her early forties, she was tall, blonde, and intelligent — but her pleasant countenance and graceful stride belied her no-nonsense demeanor. Even Angelo Belli, who worked for a major law

73

firm in the next county, and had never met her before, knew about her straight-from-the-shoulder reputation.

The judge eased herself into a large, well-upholstered chair and began to examine two citations on her desk as Belli and I took our seats. They spelled out the criminal charges against Alec Callahan, and after reviewing them, she read the charges aloud and asked Callahan how he would plea.

I glanced over at his table and watched him voice the only words he would utter through the entire trial: "Not guilty, Your Honor."

Although Alec Callahan had always denied shooting the bear at his camp, he refused to take the stand in his own defense. Instead, his attorney planned to do what all good defense attorneys do: put the police officer on trial in place of their client. Thus, everything the lawman did or didn't do is scrutinized in hope that some fatal flaw in legal procedure will emerge that sets their client free. Never mind the facts. What becomes important is whether the officer has dotted all his i's and crossed all his t's.

They say the best *defense* is a good *offense*, and I often wondered if the adage hadn't been born in the halls of Harvard Law School or some other breeding ground for defense attorneys. Alec Callahan didn't have to mutter a single syllable in order to defend himself (although I often wondered if a judge ever assumes some level of guilt upon defendants choosing to remain mum when faced with criminal charges). In a court of law, Mr. Callahan was considered innocent until proven guilty beyond a reasonable doubt. Period. And that put the onus squarely on my shoulders.

Belli suspected that I had a considerable amount of solid physical evidence against his client; consequently, his plan was to attack how I obtained it. The attorney had tipped his hand in the conference room: He would argue that my warrantless search was unlawful, and then declare that any evidence discovered at Callahan's camp must subsequently be suppressed. But first, he would have to wade through Forensic Specialist Jim LeMay's expert testimony regarding

DNA evidence. Whittle away at it, make it look flimsy, maybe even get lucky and have it thrown out on a technicality.

It was my job to see that it didn't happen.

"Is the Commonwealth ready?" asked Judge Robinson glancing my way.

"Yes, Your Honor," I replied. "The Commonwealth calls Deputy Jeff Pierce."

I wanted Pierce to testify first because he'd been the first one to visit Callahan's camp. It was his initial discovery of the blood and bait that had started everything in motion. He got up from his chair, walked over to Judge Robinson's desk, and was sworn in. Then he faced the courtroom and sat in a straight-backed wooden chair to her immediate right.

Trying to keep things brief and to the point, I asked Pierce a few specific questions about the bloody leaves and bait he discovered at Callahan's camp, and the gut pile he found later. Just enough to illustrate for the judge why he went there and what he had seen that night. When I finished, Belli stood from his chair for his opportunity to cross-examine Pierce. I expected a lengthy interrogation, but instead he asked him one simple question: Did he have a search warrant when he entered Callahan's property? When Pierce said he did not, Angelo Belli thanked him for his answer and sat down.

"No further questions, Your Honor," he said. It was his way of summarily dismissing the deputy's testimony. Telling the judge that nothing Pierce had said amounted to a hill of beans. Because without a search warrant, we had no case.

I took the stand next and testified at length about seizing Callahan's bear from his residence, the blood samples submitted to the Fish & Wildlife Forensics Lab, the bullet trajectory analysis performed on the carcass, and the statements he made to me after I had Mirandized him. I entered a dozen evidence photographs into court during my testimony, including those taken during the bullet trajectory analysis, and others taken at Callahan's camp showing the bait, bloody leaves, bear footprint, and the gut pile.

In return, Angelo Belli asked me myriad questions in a spirited attempt to trip me up, but he finally abandoned the notion and I returned to my desk to call Forensics Specialist Jim LeMay as my next witness.

After being duly sworn, LeMay took the stand and answered questions I put forward concerning his background in forensic science so I could have him certified as an expert witness in Judge Robinson's court. LeMay testified about his degree in medical technology, his years of experience with the Fish and Wildlife Service, his coauthored publications, and his professional presentations regarding DNA and forensics. The scientist's impressive list of credentials went on and on, seemingly without end, until Angelo Belli finally stood and announced to the court that he would stipulate to LeMay's expertise. Judge Robinson concurred, and granted that Jim LeMay would be considered an expert in DNA and forensic science in her courtroom.

Now it was time to get down to business. Show the court what forensic science was all about, and establish not only beyond a reasonable doubt, but to the verge of a mathematical certainty, that Callahan's bear had been shot by the bait at his camp, and not a quarter mile away as he claimed.

Taking three manila evidence envelopes from my desktop, I walked over to the witness stand and commenced my direct examination:

"Mr. LeMay," I began, "I want to show you what has been marked as Commonwealth Exhibit Numbers One, Two, and Three, and ask you to identify them for the Court."

LeMay: "These are the three envelopes containing items that I analyzed for the Pennsylvania Game Commission."

Wasserman: "And could you tell the Court what you found?"

LeMay: "The envelope marked *Item One* contained a mixture of blood on leaves, a very small piece of muscle tissue, and a single black hair [all discovered near the bait at Callahan's camp]. The envelope marked *Item Two* contained another piece of muscle tissue [taken from Callahan's bear carcass]. And then envelope marked *Number Three* contained a large piece of liver tissue [taken from the gut pile]."

Wasserman: "And what type of examination did you perform?"

LeMay: "First, I extracted DNA from all three of the evidence items. I then determined the species for each of the items using mitochondrial DNA analysis. Next, I used Short Tandem Repeat (STR) analysis to determine how many individuals were represented by the three evidence items."

Wasserman: "And could you tell the court what the results were?"

LeMay: "Yes. The species determination identified all of the three individual items as originating from a North American black bear, and the STR analysis confirmed that all three items originated from the same individual North American black bear."

Wasserman: "Thank you, Mr. LeMay. I have no further questions."

LeMay had summed it up nicely. In just a few brief sentences, his testimony validated my belief that Callahan had shot his bear next to the apple pomace at his camp, and then gutted the carcass back in the woods where Pierce had discovered the entrails. With my direct examination concluded, Angelo Belli stepped from his chair to cross-examine LeMay. He was purposefully brief, in what I considered a shallow attempt to make the scientist's findings appear insignificant and worthy of little regard. Judge Robinson didn't fall for it.

Belli: "Mr. LeMay, you don't have any expertise in terms of ballistics [bullet trajectory analysis], do you?"

LeMay: "No, I do not."

Belli: "And you're not here to testify as to *when* the bear was killed, are you?"

LeMay: "I don't believe so."

Belli: "Your only testimony here today is that these three samples that were sent to you by the Game

Commission all sort of came from the same bear that apparently is dead, is that correct?"

LeMay: "Correct."

Belli: "I have no further questions, Judge."

The Court: (Judge Robinson addressing Jim LeMay) "I have one question because the attorney just said, 'all sort of came from the same bear.' But what we're talking about here is a precise science where you are able to testify in this courtroom that those three items that were sent to you . . . without any question . . . or within a certain degree of certainty . . . came from the same bear. Well, what degree of certainty? Do you know?"

LeMay: "I can't give you a degree of certainty, Your Honor, but I can give you a probability of identity. And that probability of identity is — we use a very conservative statistical analysis to determine this — that there is a one-in-ten-thousand chance that there might be another individual black bear in this state that exhibits that same profile."

The Court: "*Very* conservative . . . ?"

LeMay: "Yes, Your Honor."

The Court: "Now, is there any redirect, any additional questions for this gentleman? He came a long way to make that statement."

She was right. LeMay *had* come a long way. Clean across the country, as a matter of fact. And I guess I should have taken more time with the man when I had him on the stand in the first place. "Yes, Your Honor," I declared. "I have additional questions."

The Court: "Proceed, officer."

Wasserman: "So what you're saying, in essence, is that all three items came from the same bear?"

LeMay: "Correct."

Wasserman: "And the probability is . . . ?"

LeMay: "One in ten thousand?"

Wasserman: "Do you recall my conversation with you earlier today when I told you what the bear population of Pennsylvania happens to be?"

LeMay: "Yes. Fifteen thousand."

Wasserman: "Now could you tell the court — just to add some additional insight regarding your agency — a little about the kind of work your laboratory does?"

LeMay: "We work on a wide variety of different species throughout the world. Ten percent of our casework is international; we get a lot of items that come through ports of entry into the United States — exotic species from Africa or Asia, etc. We work, of course, with all the big game animals of North America, and they're constantly brought in for species identification. We have also done forensic analysis for all fifty states."

Wasserman: "Thank you, Mr. LeMay. The Commonwealth rests, Your Honor."

The trial had run all morning long, and now it would come down to a final summation argument by the prosecution and the defense. It would be our last shot at persuading the judge to see things our way, although Belli and I both realized that she had most likely already come to a conclusion by now. But there was a glimmer of hope in each of us that whatever we said in these final minutes might snatch victory from the jaws of defeat. For neither of us knew which side she favored.

The defense always addresses the court first in summation argument, and when Judge Robinson called Angelo Belli for his final words, he pulled a document from his briefcase and stood fencepost straight. Then he read aloud Article one, Section eight, of the Pennsylvania Constitution, and stated that the Declaration of Rights therein provided that Alec Callahan was free from unreasonable searches and seizures, and that he had an expectation of privacy in his clearly posted property. Hence, the attorney maintained that all evidence discovered by the Game Commission should be suppressed due to the lack of a search warrant.

In return, I stood from my chair and argued that section 901 of the Pennsylvania Game and Wildlife Code states that any officer whose duty it is to investigate any alleged violations of the Code shall have the power and duty to go upon any land, outside of buildings, posted or otherwise, in the performance of his duty. As a result, we did not need a search warrant to enter Callahan's posted property. His cabin, certainly. But not his property.

"Your Honor," I continued, "in this very court, you have heard two similar cases in recent years. By coincidence, both violations also occurred in Windham Township. In *Commonwealth v. Clod*, which took place on the first day of bear season in 1994, the defendant had killed a bear 800 feet from a baited camp very similar to the scenario in the case at hand. As you may recall, Mr. Clod was convicted in this court and he subsequently appealed to the Court of Common Pleas, where your conviction was upheld by Judge Brendan Vanston. Again, Clod appealed, this time to the Commonwealth Court of Pennsylvania, where his conviction was affirmed by a panel of three judges.

"And in *Commonwealth v Sabatto*, the defendant was convicted for hunting 1000 feet from a pile of apples he'd placed at his camp during deer season. Mr. Sabatto subsequently appealed your decision to the Court of Common Pleas, where it was upheld by Judge Vanston. Like Clod, Sabatto took his appeal to the Commonwealth Court of Pennsylvania, where his conviction was also affirmed by the higher court.

"And now we have Mr. Callahan," I said, "who claims to have been hunting 1600 feet from his camp — a camp that he deliberately baited to attract game. What if it were so? What if we never considered the blood evidence found at the bait or the DNA proof offered at this trial today? What if we took him at his word — that he killed the bear away from his property — in the woods, by the end of the dirt road, 1600 feet from the bait? Would another 600 feet make any difference whatsoever? The Commonwealth thinks not.

"Your Honor," I said in conclusion, "I submit to you that surely Mr. Callahan would have been taking willful advantage of the bait he put out to attract bears by shooting one only 1600 feet away, just as Sabatto had done at 1000 feet and Clod at 800 feet."

I sat down. There was nothing else I could do. In my heart of hearts, I was convinced that Alec Callahan had killed his bear from the balcony of his cabin, and that our subsequent search of his posted property was legal by virtue of the power and authority granted under our state game laws. But none of that mattered now. The only thing that did matter is what the judge thought. Had I convinced her beyond a reasonable doubt that Callahan was guilty? Or would she rule in favor of the defendant? I tried to read her as she sat busily sorting through the notes she had taken, but she left me no clue.

Soon she paused and looked up at the attorney for a long moment, her expression vacant. Then her eyes withdrew from him and set dead level on Alec Callahan. "I've made my decision," she said glancing my way briefly before fixing a penetrating gaze on the defendant once more. "Mr. Callahan, you have chosen to remain silent while the Game Commission has presented testimony from two officers and a forensics expert that traveled 3000 miles to be here. There is absolutely no doubt in my mind that you are guilty. The officers testified that you admitted putting bait at your camp to attract wild animals. Then you killed a bear which you told them was 1600 feet away from the bait when you shot it, while we sat here and listened to Mr. LeMay testify that the blood and muscle tissue discovered at your camp came from that same bear."

Now Judge Robinson's eyes cooled as they focused on Attorney Belli. "Counselor," she said, "I've taken into consideration your argument that the officers should have had a search warrant before entering Mr. Callahan's property, and that you think the evidence they discovered should be suppressed. I disagree. The Pennsylvania Game and Wildlife Code clearly and specifically allows these officers to enter private property in the performance of their duty. Therefore, in addition to the $1000 fine and court costs imposed as a penalty, I am ordering the defendant to pay $800 to the Commonwealth in restitution for the replacement value of a black bear, plus an additional $1500 in costs to cover Mr. LeMay's airfare from Oregon."

Angelo Belli's jaw tightened briefly, then he slowly closed his briefcase and stood. "Thank you, Your Honor," he nodded.

It was a matter of courtesy and respect that he said that; and I knew it had to be difficult for him to accept the fact that he had lost to a civil servant unpracticed in criminal law. But I also knew that we would meet again, this time in a higher court. And when we did, Angelo Belli would be much better prepared after his "trial run" with Judge Robinson. For now he knew who my witnesses were and what their testimony would reveal. Appeals take months, even years sometimes, before they're scheduled for a new hearing. And in that time, memories can become cloudy. Witnesses are vulnerable when they can't remember clearly. Their uncertainty draws the defense attorney in like blood to a hungry shark. And he hammers away at them, shouting sometimes; demanding answers to questions he knows they can't answer, no matter the insignificance; thus, compounding their bewilderment until their credibility begins to fall apart. An experienced criminal defense attorney can see it coming from a mile away. He can smell their fear. And he lives for it.

Angelo Belli must have stopped by the county courthouse to file for an appeal on his way back to the office that same day, because before I knew it, a trial date had been set at the Wyoming County Court of Common Pleas. We were in November, my busiest time of the year, so I had to wait until after deer season ended before I could begin preparing for the trial. It would be heard *de novo*, a Latin term meaning anew or over again, and refers to the appellate court's authority to hear the evidence of a case without reference to the prior court's interpretation or application of the law.

Belli knew the strengths and weaknesses of my case now. And he was well aware that the DNA evidence and bullet trajectory analysis I had done would put Callahan's bear directly on top of the bait when it was shot. That he would file a motion to suppress the evidence was a certainty. It was his best shot at a win. And because his request would be considered anew, by a judge who may well have an opinion entirely different from Judge Robinson's, I feared that his motion might be granted.

The defense attorney didn't disappoint me. A legal brief outlining his request to have evidence suppressed was initiated long before the trial began. It encompassed everything discovered at Callahan's camp: the bait, the bloody leaves and muscle tissue, the DNA evidence, the bear footprint in the apple pomace, and all physical measurements obtained on the property. Everything would be lost if the judge granted his request. And because Belli's argument for suppression was based on extensive research he'd done on constitutional law regarding search and seizure, I felt compelled to come up with some case law of my own that supported a warrantless entry into Callahan's property.

However, I soon found that legal research can be mind-boggling as I attempted to wade through the thousands of state and federal legal filings on public record, hoping to unearth something analogous to my case. Fortunately, I knew someone who could help me: Attorney Stanley Cohen, founder and publisher of the *Pennsylvania Police Criminal Law Bulletin* (a monthly publication for police officers and police law services).

I had met Mr. Cohen years ago, and found him to be extremely knowledgeable about case law on search and seizure, as well as interrogation and other police-related matters. He is widely known and respected as someone who has dedicated his life to helping police officers, and he agreed to assist me with my case. Mr. Cohen managed to find several high court decisions in favor of warrantless searches that paralleled the Callahan case, and he elaborated on these judicial precedents for me, going into considerable detail as to how they could be used to argue against Angelo Belli's motion to suppress my evidence.

One particular case involved a police officer who entered private property to investigate a car theft. Cohen explained that entering private property without a warrant to investigate an anonymous tip of a crime has been considered lawful and proper by many appellate courts, and that once the officer is on the property, he may seize evidence that he sees in plain view, outside of buildings, without a warrant.

Armed with the information provided by Mr. Cohen, I felt confident that the evidence discovered at Callahan's camp would not be suppressed, and forwarded his findings to the district attorney's office along with all documents and photographs pertaining to the case. Because the trial would be heard at the county courthouse, it became the DA's responsibility to prosecute it for me.

This is not always good news. Some district attorneys are so busy dealing with murders, rapes, and other serious felonies, they have neither the time nor the inclination to be bothered with wildlife crimes — especially when they're considered mere summary offenses. Earlier in my career, while stationed in a heavily populated county near Philadelphia, the best I could hope for was a quick 15-minute review of my case, just before the trial, by an overworked assistant district attorney in the midst of a dozen other hearings scheduled for the same day. But Wyoming County was a rural mountainous area that lacked the chaotic caseload of big city crime districts. Hunting was a way of life here. Bear poaching: headline news. Hence, an affable and diligent prosecutor in his mid-thirties was assigned to my case.

Assistant District Attorney Jerry Idec greeted me with a robust handshake as I stepped into his office to brief him on my investigation. Standing six feet tall with a sinewy frame and boyish good looks, he wore a neatly pressed white shirt and navy tie loosened at the neck. Idec's reputation for diving enthusiastically into his work became immediately evident. He asked dozens of questions about the case, his curious eyes wide and comprehending as I related the events leading up to Alec Callahan's arrest. We sat for more than an hour, and when the interview ended, Idec surprised me by asking if I would take him to the crime scene. "It's not often I get to work on poaching cases," he said. "This one really intrigues me. I'd like to look around, get a better idea of what actually happened out there."

"When would you like to go?" I asked.

Idec glanced at his wristwatch. "I have an appointment later this afternoon. How about right now?"

When we returned from Callahan's property, Attorney Idec wasted no time getting down to business. Within a matter of days he contacted me by telephone to say that Angelo Belli would stipulate to the DNA evidence against Callahan. Belli knew he couldn't shake Jim Lemay's testimony, and he didn't want to risk getting stuck with another bill for his airfare. But he never intended to let that evidence be heard either; hence, his motion to suppress it due to our lack of a search warrant. In response, Idec composed a lengthy, thorough, and well-argued brief in opposition to the defense attorney's motion, and submitted it to Judge Brendan J. Vanston.

Belli had hoped that the judge would rule on his motion prior to the trial and render a decision mandating that my blood evidence be thrown out. Had Judge Vanston obliged him, my case against Alec Callahan would have been struck a severe blow, and perhaps ended then and there. But, interestingly, the judge chose to hear testimony about the case before making his decision.

MARCH 31, 2003.

Built in 1843, the Wyoming County Courthouse is a stately, three-story Italianate style building constructed of brick and white stucco with tall arched windows and heavy, ornate knee braces to support the massive overhanging eves of the roof. Inside, the sprawling second-story wood-paneled courtroom was no less impressive as I sat with Attorney Idec awaiting Judge Vanston's entrance.

Although the judge wasn't a hunter, he owned a few assorted firearms and enjoyed target shooting. He also harbored a fond appreciation for wildlife. Consequently, most game law violations were not regarded as trivial matters in his court. Of medium height and slender build with a broad forehead, discerning eyes, and a neatly trimmed mustache, Judge Vanston looked more like a distinguished intellectual than a no-nonsense arbiter of justice. As a former district attorney, he had been an aggressive prosecutor, securing convictions on scores of lawbreakers. As a judge, Vanston took his uncompromising pursuit of justice directly into the courtroom, where convicted criminals received swift and just punishment. But the judge also had a keen sense of humor about him and would often use his razor-sharp wit to interject levity into the courtroom when a case became tedious or to temper the bickering between rival attorneys.

My heart thumped when the Courtroom Crier strode into the room, for I knew things were about to get started. Everything depended on the assistant district attorney now, and the grim notion that the case could be won or lost solely by how he conducted himself in court had me feeling a bit uneasy. Actually, powerless would be a better way to describe it, for unlike in summary court with Judge Robinson, I was no longer the chief prosecutor, but rather a mere witness for the Commonwealth. And courtroom procedure dictated that I not utter a word unless asked a question by an attorney or the judge — I couldn't speak unless spoken to. Consequently, if Attorney Idec forgot to bring up something crucial to the case while I was on the witness stand, it could spell disaster.

— *"ALL RISE!"* announced the Crier in a powerful baritone, and we all rose from our seats to stand iron rod straight as a black-robed judge stepped into the chamber before us. He walked directly to his imposing mahogany bench — situated strategically as the highest place in the room — and looked at no one before settling into a large and comfortable looking leather chair. Now the Crier spoke again, but in a much lower tone: "You may be seated!" he declared, allowing everyone to finally settle into their own chairs. Idec and I sat side-by-side at a roomy wooden desk positioned 20 feet from the judge. A short distance behind us a similar desk accommodated Angelo Belli and Alec Callahan, and at a distance behind them, two wooden benches stretched the width of the courtroom for any spectators who might wish to observe the proceedings.

And now the judge addressed the room: "Good morning," he nodded briefly. "All right, we have a summary appeal, Mr. Callahan, for game law violations — and there's also a motion to suppress evidence. I think the best way to do it is to hear all the evidence and sort it out afterwards; it just makes a lot more sense that way." He paused for a moment, as if waiting for someone to voice an objection, then said, "Idec, go ahead . . ."

In order to establish a foundation for the case, the assistant district attorney called Deputy Pierce as his first witness. Through Idec's questioning, Pierce was able to paint a clear picture for the judge, depicting Callahan's camp and the surrounding terrain, as well as explain the circumstances leading up to his inspection of the property and subsequent discovery of the bait, the bloody leaves, and the gut pile.

Immediately after Idec finished questioning Pierce, the tenacious Angelo Belli began his cross-examination, attacking the deputy with a vengeance. But Pierce managed to hold his own, and after being bombarded with questions and accusations for the better part of an hour, the beleaguered deputy finally stepped down from the witness chair, prompting Judge Vanston to order a five-minute recess.

Taking advantage of the lull in proceedings, I stood to stretch my legs and glanced toward the spectator bench only to spy the poacher Joe Gunner seated there with another man. There were no other observers, just these two. Both men glared at me with contempt as I ambled over to my deputy and complemented him on a job well done.

"See who's back there?" grumbled Pierce.

I nodded. "Who's the other guy?"

"I don't know," Pierce shrugged. "But I'll bet a dollar to a donut both of 'em helped Callahan take his bear. Just wish we could prove it."

I smiled briefly. "Every dog has his day!"

But inside, my guts were churning. Inside, I knew that every dog really didn't have his day — and my deputy's face told me he knew it too. Poachers vastly outnumber game wardens. Truth is, every so often we get lucky and catch somebody, that's all. Had an informant not called to report Callahan's baited camp we wouldn't even be here today. How's that for catching bad guys?

I looked back at Gunner and his companion, my gaze deliberate as arrows. And as their eyes fell, I turned slowly and walked back to my chair.

When Judge Vanston revisited his bench, Attorney Idec called me to the witness stand where I was promptly sworn in. After answering a few standard questions for the court reporter, like how to spell my name and who I worked for, Idec began questioning me in detail. Step by step, we methodically introduced our evidence against Callahan: the DNA confirmation of the blood and tissue samples, measurements obtained at his camp, photographs of the bait and the gut pile, how the evidence was preserved, chain of custody, and so on. Everything went along smoothly too. That is, until Idec questioned me about the photograph depicting a bear track in the apple pomace. That's when Belli saw an opportunity to strike, and he jumped in with both feet. The testimony went like this:

Idec: ". . . And in what direction was the track pointing?"

Wasserman: "Away from Mr. Callahan's cabin toward the gut pile we discovered at the end of the woods road."

Idec: "Based on your experience, when a bear is startled which way does it run in relation to where it was in the first place?" —

Belli: "Objection!"

The Court: (Judge Vanston) "Sustained. Idec, you're going to have to establish experience on this one."

Idec: "Officer Wasserman, how many years experience do you have as a state game warden?"

Wasserman: "Thirty years."

Idec: "What about prior to that, when did you start having an interest in wildlife?"

Wasserman: "I first developed an interest in wildlife at age five. When I got a little older, I began hunting and trapping, which led into a lifetime of studying animal tracks and animal behavior. I've continued to educate myself about wildlife for the past 50 years."

Idec: "Have you had occasion to learn about bears?"

Wasserman: "Yes. I trap and relocate nuisance bears as a routine part of my job each year. You develop an intimate knowledge about an animal when you're trying to lure it into a trap. Bears are a lot like children: Gullible. Trusting. Playful. They like sweets too. Just like kids. That's why the sweet aroma of fermenting apples is so attractive to them."

Idec: (Confident that my background would be sufficient for the court.) "Now, back to the fact that the footprint was pointed away from the cabin, toward the entrails. Generally, how do bears take off if they're startled?"

Belli: "The same objection, Your Honor."

The Court: "The objection is overruled. But it goes to weight, not admissibility. You may answer the question."

But it goes to weight, not admissibility. I wasn't entirely sure what the judge meant by that, other than that it spelled bad news for the defense — and I began to think that the judge had a keen interest in the case. I cut my eyes toward Alec Callahan; he was sitting next to his attorney, fingers laced on the desktop in front of him. He gazed back at me in a detached sort of way, as if he hadn't a care in the world.

I answered Idec's question: "With few exceptions, a bear — like any other startled animal — will run in the opposite direction from whatever frightens it. That's just normal animal behavior."

Idec: "In your experience are you familiar with scents and lures with regard to animals?"

Wasserman: "Yes."

Idec: "Is apple pomace something that would attract bears?"

Belli: (Standing abruptly now, his brow contracted into a wrinkled scowl.) "I'm going to object, Judge. He has no specialized knowledge in terms of this! There's no wildlife expert here, and I object to this testimony. He's just a game warden! If they have a wildlife PhD or something like that, well, okay then, but — "

The Court: "I have to tell you that in a similar proceeding, several years ago, Dr. Gary Alt, the world renowned bear expert, sat here [in this courtroom] and told me that apples are a bear attractant (See: *Poacher Wars, Incident at Dutch Mountain*), so I have that knowledge in my head. I can't dismiss it. And it's common knowledge anyway. Overruled! You can answer the question, officer: Do apples attract bears?"

Wasserman: "Apples do attract bears, especially in the fall when Mr. Callahan's bear was shot. They're consuming up to twenty thousand calories per day preparing for hibernation."

Belli's face had melted into a momentary look of despair when Judge Vanston acknowledged his prior experience with a bear baiting case where apples were used. Nevertheless, the defense lawyer had plenty of fight left in him, and as Idec continued to question me about the case, he barked at his heels at every opportunity. But the judge, apparently desiring to hear my story, overruled most of his objections — much to the dismay of Joe Gunner and his bonehead companion who had been squirming in their seats in the back of the courtroom, snickering and hissing at each other throughout most of the trial.

The judge finally had enough.

"You two!" he called out. "Could you either . . . it's distracting! I understand the seats are hard but you either have to stay or leave — but you can't be fidgeting around. It makes the sheriff nervous, okay?"

Judge Vanston, clearly agitated, was being immensely polite considering their clownish behavior. Though his words were gracious, there had been a noticeably ominous tone to his voice. A final warning so to speak. And the men, detecting this, sat frozen in their seats for the remainder of the trial.

When Attorney Idec's direct examination about the DNA evidence and the bait at Callahan's cabin drew to a conclusion, he began asking me questions about the bullet trajectory analysis I had performed on the defendant's bear. Attorney Belli objected vehemently, pointing out that I had no accredited training or certification in forensic ballistics. "Judge," he protested, "I make a motion that he not be allowed to testify. He's unqualified!"

But Judge Vanston wasn't entirely convinced. "It's not clear to me how specific or how general his testimony will be," he replied. "I'll let it proceed. But you can move to strike it when he's concluded with that portion of his evidence."

Idec managed to get everything in: how we propped the bear on skids to reproduce its natural height when it was shot; how the bullet came from in front of the bear, at a high angle over its head, entering its back between the shoulder and vertebrae — illustrating that the animal could not have been shot broadside as Callahan claimed; how we had used an iron rod to trace the bullet's path, including photographs of the rod jutting from the carcass to demonstrate the trajectory; photographs of Callahan's cabin depicting the balcony and the apple pomace below; and lastly, how someone shooting from level ground would have to be standing directly in front of the bear, a mere ten feet away, for a bullet to travel through the carcass at the angle Callahan's bullet had.

When I finished my testimony the defense made a motion to strike (disallow) it. Judge Vanston denied the motion — with the exception that my testimony regarding my conclusions about the bullet trajectory analysis would not be allowed. But I didn't mind. We managed to get it all in, and the judge was more than capable of making his own conclusions.

Having managed to introduce all our evidence against Alec Callahan, Idec rested his case, spurring the judge to call another five-minute recess. The courtroom cleared out quickly. We had been at it for almost two hours, and everyone headed for the lavatories down the hall. Everyone except me. For I chose to remain in my seat, savoring the peacefulness of the empty room.

The calm before the storm.

Now Angelo Belli would have his chance to cross-examine me. And I would be held accountable for everything I did, as well as everything I didn't do, during my investigation. Truth is, *I* would be the person on trial today, not Alec Callahan. Callahan didn't have to take the stand — didn't have to say a word to defend himself. Instead, the trial would focus on me. And everything I said or didn't say would be held against me in court at every conceivable opportunity. It's ironic, but that's how our judicial system works. Alec Callahan's conviction, first and foremost, would hinge directly upon whether or not *I* was "found guilty": Did I have authority to enter Callahan's property without a search warrant? Did I question him without administering his right to remain silent? Did I intimidate him, coerce him, persuade him in any way? Did I follow proper chain-of-custody procedures? — My motives, and yes, even my thoughts, would be questioned and held to suspicion as the defense attorney methodically probed me like some obscure new specimen under a microscope in his attempt to show that I was guilty of some wrongdoing in order to get his client off the hook.

And so, as the recess ended and the courtroom began to show life again, a sense of dread settled over me. Not the paralyzing dread one might find if he were plummeting toward earth with a locked parachute, but a more subtle *I'm going to hate this!* kind of dread — like when you're lying on a cold examination table wearing nothing but a flimsy medical gown, and the proctologist snaps on his rubber glove. You want to jump up. Walk out of the room. But you know you can't, so you prepare yourself for what's coming.

When Judge Vanston called on the defense attorney to begin his cross-examination, Angelo Belli placed both hands on his desk, rose slowly from his chair, and walked all the way across the courtroom floor until he stood directly in front of me. He wore an impeccable double-breasted suit — jet-black like his trademark ponytail. He was close enough to touch. And for a long, agonizing moment, he said nothing. Just stood there, jaw rigid, blue eyes staring at me icily — calculatingly.

Then, as if a light switch went off in his head, I watched his sun-bronzed face began to soften. And a faint smile broke across his lips. A self-satisfied smile. A smile that seemed to say, *I'm gonna enjoy tearing you apart!*

Lacing his fingers together, he exhaled slowly before asking his opening question, — a question he knew I could only answer *yes* to — the key to winning his case in court: "Mr. Wasserman," he began, "I'm going to ask you first about November 19th: Isn't it true that you didn't have a search warrant when you searched Mr. Callahan's property that day?"

He called me *Mister* Wasserman. I chuckled inside. Defense attorneys would often address me as *mister* rather than *officer* during cross-examination hoping their casual disregard for my position as a law enforcement officer would rattle my cage a little. Tweak my emotions. Make their job easy. It never worked. But I'd be lying if I didn't admit that it annoyed me a little.

"Yes," I said, answering his question while knowing full well that it would be first blood for him. The search warrant issue was the ugly black eye in my case. Belli had landed his first blow, and like a prizefighter looking for a title shot, he'd start pounding away now, hoping to bring me down.

"And you didn't even try to get a search warrant, did you?" he crowed.

"No," I said.

"And when you went on that property you saw signs posted that say *No Trespassing*, isn't that correct?"

"Yes."

"And they were clear as day, correct?"

"Yes."

"And would you agree with me that you've been on that property before — several times, in fact?"

"Yes."

"And every time you went on that property, you saw those clearly posted signs that say *No Trespassing*, isn't that correct?"

"Yes."

"And when you were there you also saw a cable going across the roadway to Mr. Callahan's property, correct?"

"Yes."

"And you walked over that, correct?"

"Yes."

"And you never asked Mr. Callahan for any kind of permission to go on his property, correct?"

"Correct," I said.

Belli paused and stared at me quizzically, as if he'd been expecting more. Some stammering perhaps, as I attempted in a vein to defend my actions. But unlike Angelo Belli, I never thought my lack of a search warrant meant much of anything. The evidence had been in plain view, in an open area, away from Callahan's cabin. Why would I need one?

But to Angelo Belli the search warrant was everything. And clearly, I stood to lose on that single issue alone if Judge Vanston agreed with him.

Satisfied he had made his point, he placed both hands on the wooden railing separating us and leaned in for his next question: "Now," he said with an arched brow, "regarding the information you received about Mr. Callahan's camp being baited . . . who gave that to you?"

It was a question that I knew he would ask. But the information had come from a confidential informant. Someone who had pleaded with me not involve them. I remembered the voice on the phone, hesitant, fearful — *Look...I don't want to get involved any further in this, I...I'm afraid of retaliation...*

And then my own words came back to haunt me. My promise: *Don't worry. You won't be involved. You've got my word on that —*

"WELL...WHO WAS IT?" boomed the defense attorney.

I glared back at him. What difference did it make? The informant's name wouldn't help him win his case. What did he want it for, so his client would have a name to dwell on — someone to hate? Someone to settle a score with?

Idec tried to head him off. "Objection! Relevancy!" he cried.

"Overruled," declared the judge.

I was stunned. Now the judge wanted a name — or at least thought it appropriate that the defense should have it. And Judge Vanston wasn't someone to defy during a trial.

I looked at the district attorney. Grim faced, he shrugged submissively and nodded for me to answer.

I cut my eyes back to Belli — gleeful, his head in the air — and I felt my jaw set with conviction.

"I don't remember," I said.

"You don't remember...!" Belli's voice was acid.

"No."

"Is that your testimony here today?"

"It is."

The lawyer turned abruptly, strode back to his desk, and retrieved his stenographer's transcript of the first trial. "Do you remember testifying at the hearing with District Justice Robinson, when I asked you the same question, and your answer to the question was, 'I'm not going to tell you,' because you thought it was protected information?"

"Yes," I said.

"So your testimony today is that you forgot the name of the person between the time that we had the hearing with the district justice and our court trial today — is that correct?"

"No. That's not correct."

"Well! What then?" he barked.

"I forgot the name long before the district justice hearing," I said. "My informant didn't want to be involved. I respected that. So, there was no reason for me to remember any name. When you asked for the informant's name at the summary trial, I objected on the grounds of relevancy, and my objection was sustained by Judge Robinson. The issue was vacated. I didn't have to explain anything more to you. Now you're asking me the same question today, and the objection by Attorney Idec has been overruled. So I'm compelled to answer, and I'm telling you I don't remember the name. I didn't remember it then, and I don't remember it now."

And then came the ugly, mocking, accusatory question that every trial lawyer loves to ask when they are caught off guard and can't think of anything else to do but cast doubt on your answer — essentially, they call you a liar:

"You understand you're under oath here today — right?" he leveled at me.

Oh, I understood all right. I understood a lot of things. Just like I understood from day one that I might be required to give up my informant's name in court. So I had put it out of my mind almost immediately (Regrettably, forgetting things like someone's name seemed to be getting easier with each passing year.). What Angelo Belli *didn't* understand is that I'd never lower myself into the cesspool of blatant thieves and liars that I had dedicated my life to apprehending; and when I raised my hand in court and swore to tell the truth, it actually meant something. And what Belli didn't *know* was that someone in the courtroom actually did remember the informant's name: Deputy Pierce, unlike me, had a memory like a steel trap. He never forgot details — especially names. But Angelo Belli had never asked Pierce for the informant's name when he questioned him in front of

Judge Robinson several months ago, just like he had failed to ask him in front of Judge Vanston when he had him on the stand earlier today. And so I answered his question unreservedly and with a clear conscience: "Yes," I said. "I understand."

Belli raised a dubious brow, and I watched the ghost of a smile flash across his chiseled face.

Touché!

He had presumed that I'd cunningly managed to dodge his question by claiming a lack of memory. And, ironically, his expression conveyed a look of genuine respect for me now — as if I had suddenly been deemed a worthy opponent. He wouldn't push it any further. I had won this round. It was time to move on.

Continuing his interrogation, Belli questioned me with a robust enthusiasm as he attempted to raise doubts about my previous testimony. He reminded the court that I lacked certification in the forensic ballistics, implying therefore, that my bullet trajectory analysis was worthless. He brought out the fact that I had never been certified as an expert in bullet wounds, casting skepticism upon my statements regarding exit and entrance wounds, and how to distinguish between the two. He grilled me on the DNA evidence: how it was collected, preserved, transported. And he hammered away at the notion that the apples found in the stomach of his client's bear could have come from a local apple orchard located on the other side of the woods — that the animal may never have set foot on Callahan's property in the first place. Then, finally, he got to the most important issue of all: the blood that would bring dishonor upon his client and ensure his conviction in court.

"Now," he said, "you have testified that blood was found on leaves by the apple pomace, correct?"

"Yes."

"And the blood was dry, correct?"

"Yes."

"Couldn't those leaves have blown from the gut pile over to where the apple pomace was?" insisted Belli. He glanced at the judge, trying to read his face.

You've got to be kidding! I thought. I couldn't help but wince at the absurdity of his question.

"Not really," I said.

"Leaves can't blow that far . . . ?"

"Not *those* leaves."

"And what do you base that on?"

"First," I began, "there's a huge tract of woods separating the apple pomace from the gut pile — a barrier of maple, oak, and beech trees that make your suggestion not even remotely possible. Secondly, the leaves were flattened, matted, not loose on the property as if they'd recently touched down. They'd been there awhile. I had to peel them off the ground."

"And that's based on what kind of training that you have?"

Belli's blatant disregard for my background as a hunter, trapper, and woodsman began to grate on me. What did he want — a college degree in leafology!

"It's based on a lifetime in the outdoors," I explained. "A lifetime of exploring nature and tracking wild animals. I mean it's just — "

Belli raised a hand and cut me off. "Yes, but do you have any training in forestry or anything like that?" he insisted.

And it was his very words, *training in forestry,* that suddenly triggered my memory. Of course! Three decades ago, I had attended Pennsylvania's one-of-a-kind academy unofficially known as the Game Commission Training School (where all newly hired officers receive 50-weeks of intensive instruction before graduating). The unwritten law for trial lawyers is not to ask a question unless you know what the answer will be. And by failing to heed that rule, Angelo Belli had given me a golden opportunity to finally shut him up.

"Yes, I've had training," I replied. "A year of training at the Ross Leffler School of Conservation where I studied forestry, dendrology, ornithology, and wildlife management before graduating as a wildlife conservation officer. I've had regular updates on these subjects over the past 30 years as well."

The attorney stared at me in slow, contemplative silence. Then he pursed his lips and nodded with grim resignation. My testimony about the leaves would stand.

Angelo Belli had hoped I would have fallen for his ludicrous isn't-it-possible scenario — that the bloody leaves at the gut pile could have been lifted by a capricious wind and carried a quarter mile over treetops only to land conveniently next to the apple pomace at his client's camp.

After all, anything is possible, isn't it?

It's an old and sometimes effective ploy, often used by defense attorneys to short-circuit a witness. Answer *yes*, and he eats your lunch.

And so the trial finally trickled to a close. It had lasted five grueling hours, and would have gone longer had Alec Callahan taken the stand in his own defense. Angelo Belli had done his best to defend him but the evidence presented against his client had been undefeatable; hence, the entire case hinged upon whether or not I had the right to enter Callahan's property without a search warrant. Belli knew this, and he argued the point vehemently in his final summation.

Although he conceded that the Pennsylvania Game and Wildlife Code granted game wardens the right to search private property without a warrant, he contended that to do so was a violation of his client's constitutional right to privacy, by virtue of the Pennsylvania Constitution. And that because the Constitution superseded state laws, my warrantless search was unlawful. He insisted therefore, that all evidence against his client should be thrown out and the case against him dismissed.

Judge Vanston wasn't so sure, and wanted to explore various courts' interpretations of the Pennsylvania

Constitution, as well as examine other case law encompassing judicial precedents regarding search and seizure, before making his decision.

Court was adjourned.

And then three weeks passed.

I was on my way out the door when I heard my office phone ring. I picked up the receiver.

"Bill, it's Jerry Idec!" He sounded excited.

"Hey! What's up?"

"Judge Vanston's decision came through today. Callahan was found guilty. Congratulations!"

"Outstanding!" I said. "But I should be congratulating *you* for the great work you did prosecuting the case."

"Nah! Just doing my job. Hey, tell you what, I'm at the office buried in paperwork; stop by and I'll give you a copy of the judge's opinion. It's seven pages!"

"I'll be right over."

Jerry was sitting at his desk, absorbed in a telephone conversation when I walked into his office. He cast a cheerful smile my way, and then rolled his eyes and shrugged apologetically. "I can't get away from this guy!" he whispered covering the mouthpiece with his hand. "Sit tight, I'll get it for you."

I smiled back at him and watched as he began to rifle through a stack of paperwork. Idec thumbed halfway through the pile before he suddenly pulled a document out and waved it in the air. "*Aha!*" he cried triumphantly.

I reached out and took it from him.

"Enjoy!" he whispered cupping the phone once again. "You deserve it."

I nodded in appreciation and stepped back outside. Jerry was a good man. A dedicated man. I felt fortunate to have had him on my side.

I didn't have to wait long to read the document. My patrol car was parked at the curb just outside Idec's office, so I hustled over and slid behind the steering wheel. Centered in large bold print on the first page were the words: ***ORDER OF COURT***. My eyes dropped to the ruling below, and I breathed a sigh of relief after seeing that Callahan had not only been found guilty on both charges, but also ordered to pay $1000 in fines plus $2,300.00 in restitution to the Pennsylvania Game Commission, essentially upholding the district court ruling made several months before. Anxious to read the judge's comments, I flipped the page and began poring over the six-page written opinion that followed.

In a nutshell, it stated that while the evidence proving Callahan's guilt had been overwhelming, the defense maintained that it was the "fruit of an illegal search," and should therefore be suppressed. But Judge Vanston found that although judicial precedents set by both the Pennsylvania Supreme Court and the U.S. Supreme Court bar warrantless searches of a person's home and the curtilage (area immediately surrounding the dwelling), he could find nothing to show that the Courts' intended to include the unoccupied or undeveloped area outside the curtilage. In his final paragraph, he stated his conclusion:

. . . the bait pile nearest the cabin is more than 90 feet from the cabin and on a tree line. The other baited areas are more distant. Based on the testimony of the officers and the photographic evidence presented, this Court concludes that the nearest bait pile is not within the curtilage of the cabin. A person standing at the bait pile would not be able to observe any activity within the cabin. Consequently, this Court concludes that the search and seizure by the Officers on November 19 and November 20, 2001 was neither unreasonable nor barred by the Constitution of Pennsylvania. Therefore, the Motion to Suppress must be denied. To rule otherwise would emasculate the enforcement of the Game Code on any privately owned realty, as one would only have to post "No Trespassing" signs to keep out

*the game wardens. Surely, the Constitutional Convention of
1968 could not have intended such an absurd result.*

I lifted my eyes from the page and squinted into the
morning sun. *No pulled punches there!* I thought. Judge
Vanston had made his feelings perfectly clear, and I couldn't
have agreed with him more.

But the persistent Alec Callahan was not done fighting,
and he immediately appealed his guilty verdict to the
Commonwealth Court of Pennsylvania where his argument
was heard before a panel of three judges. It took awhile for a
decision to come forth, but nine months later, on January 7,
2004, his guilty verdict was affirmed once again, in an
eleven-page opinion.

The judges' examination of the appeal began and ended
with Callahan's argument that the "No Trespassing" signs
posted on his property created a reasonable expectation of
privacy, and that entry by game wardens would have been
unlawful — "W*hen you went on that property you saw signs
posted that say 'No Trespassing,' isn't that correct?"* his
attorney had declared when he had me on the stand in front
of Judge Vanston. And so, in their final paragraph, the three-
judge panel concluded their analysis with the following
statement:

. . . *when we closely examine the law of trespass, we
find an* exception *to the power of posted signs, which
exception includes game officers when performing their duty.
Here, the signs, while legally placed by Callahan in an
attempt to keep unwelcome and unlawful trespassers off his
property, do not negate a game officer's right and authority
to investigate a crime scene relating to game or wildlife.
Thus Callahan's posting of the signs cannot form the basis of
a reasonable expectation of privacy; it would be
unreasonable for him to expect that game officers, who are
privileged to enter the land, would not do so to assure
compliance with the Game Law. Indeed, we agree with the
trial court that if Callahan's position were the law in our
Commonwealth, criminals could very easily carry on illegal*

enterprises by merely placing "No Trespassing" signs around the perimeter of their property.

But once again, Alec Callahan refused to accept an appellate Court's verdict, and subsequently petitioned the highest court in the Commonwealth to review his case. The Pennsylvania Supreme Court receives about 2,500 civil and criminal appeals each year; however, it generally hears only those cases that it deems to have statewide importance. As a result, relatively few game law appeals have ever been examined by the high court. Alec Callahan's would be one of them.

In three decades as a game warden with more than 1000 prosecutions under my belt, I found Alec Callahan to be one of the most tenacious fighters I ever encountered. Appeals are expensive undertakings, especially when you bring them to this level. Callahan's attorney would have to commit himself to several days work preparing a legal brief for the Court to review. Then, at some later date, both he and the Wyoming County District Attorney would be called to Philadelphia where they would argue the case in front of the seven Supreme Court Justices.

And since this was Callahan's third appeal — his third time at bat, so to speak, I had to wonder what made a man like Alec Callahan tick — a man willing to spend a small fortune in attorney fees attempting to defeat the mountain of evidence stacked against him. Was he trying to save face? Prove to himself, his friends, his family, that he could beat the warden at his own game? Perhaps so, I thought.

There was much riding on Callahan's final plea. If the Supreme Court found for the defendant, every police officer in Pennsylvania, not just game wardens, would be prohibited from entering private property on a "tip" that criminal activity was taking place unless they were armed with a search warrant.

Search warrants take time to procure. Precious time. They must be approved by a judge, the majority of whom are not available on weekends and nights (when most criminal activity occurs). And as minutes turn into hours, valuable evidence can disappear. What's more, many judges will not approve a search warrant based on information from an anonymous informant, which is problematic due to the fact that most informants wish to remain anonymous. Consequently, a ruling in favor of Alec Callahan would not only prevent warrantless game wardens from entering private property on a "tip" about illegal hunting, but would also bar the police from investigating anonymous information about a marijuana crop in an open field somewhere.

But on November 20, 2006, five years (almost to the day) after my investigation began, Alec Callahan's conviction was upheld in an exhaustively researched 25-page written opinion by the Pennsylvania Supreme Court. The seven Justices analyzed dozens of search and seizure cases, some dating back to the prohibition days of the early twenties, before making a final judgment. In conclusion, the state Supreme Court in its majority opinion penned the following statement:

The citizens of this Commonwealth throughout our history have shown a keen interest in protecting and preserving the diverse wildlife that find refuge in the fields and forests within our borders. This interest is so strong that it is enshrined by a separate provision of the Pennsylvania Constitution.

The legislative and executive branches, in turn, have enacted and executed a plethora of statutes and regulations designed to enforce the people's right to the preservation of our wildlife. Thus, our Constitution and enacted statutes — as well as the agencies created to enforce them — all confirm that, in Pennsylvania, any subjective expectation for privacy against governmental intrusion in open fields is not an expectation that our society has ever been willing to recognize as reasonable.

[Game Law] Enforcement, it is worth noting, is a monumental task. For every three hundred fifty square miles of land in Pennsylvania, only one full-time game warden is assigned to conduct wildlife protection.

In light of the foregoing, we hold that the guarantees of

Article I, Section 8 of the Pennsylvania Constitution do not extend to open fields; federal and state law, in this area, are coextensive. Therefore, we affirm the Commonwealth Court's determination that Officers Wasserman and Pierce did not violate appellant's right to be free from unreasonable searches and seizures.

And so, the case against Alec Callahan had finally come to a conclusion. His fines, the seizure of his bear, and the revocation of his hunting and trapping privileges would stand. Ironically, Callahan's tireless endeavor to overcome his conviction, and thereby prevent game wardens from entering private posted property to investigate incidents of poaching, had ensured the opposite result. Pennsylvania's thin green line of wildlife enforcement officers now had the official sanction of the Supreme Court behind them, and they had Alec Callahan to thank for it.

NOVEMBER 27, 2006

Joe Gunner stood on the balcony of his cabin under a slate gray sky and watched two figures approaching through the trees from afar. They moved toward him in a steady, purposeful gait. Dedicated men. Determined men. One in green, the other in gray.

He knew why they were coming, but it was too late. They were moving too quickly. Boots biting into the earth as they advanced. Two uniformed men striding side by side. Brothers bound in duty and honor. One a game warden, the other a state trooper.

Joe Gunner raised the glass in his hand, belted down the amber liquid, and wiped his mouth with his sleeve. It was 9:00 A.M.

As they drew close to the cabin, Deputy Pierce cuffed the trooper's chest, signaling him to stop. There was a pickup truck parked out front, and a freshly killed doe lay on the ground by the tailgate. Its sleek white belly slit open, the entrails removed. "One down," said Pierce. "Could be another one in the truck. Cover me, Jesse; I'm going to take a look."

Pierce had known the trooper for a very long time, and had watched him grow from an inquisitive, fun-loving schoolboy into a good and decent man in his mid-twenties. And although the trooper was younger and more robust, Pierce looked after him like a son. Because the truck was out in the open, he had Jesse stay back where he could seek cover if anyone started taking potshots at them.

As Pierce moved forward, the trooper's eyes scanned the cabin. Built of oak logs with a large picture window in front, he could see two men standing inside: one tall and lean, the other short and fat. They were facing each other, arguing. The taller man waving his arms frantically, the shorter man staring up at him in wooden silence.

Jesse supposed their quarrel was most likely about him and Pierce suddenly showing up on their property. Surely they had seen them coming through the open woods. And their apparent apprehension only served to make him all the more wary.

The trooper repositioned himself beside a towering oak tree thirty feet from the cabin and continued to watch them. Now he could hear the taller man's voice roaring through the window like a lion in a cave, his words laced with profanities as he paced nervously about. Because the men had access to guns, Jesse placed his palm on the hilt of his Glock and unsnapped his holster as a precaution.

The sudden thud of a tailgate dropping caused the trooper to whip his head around. The deputy looked back at him and nodded briefly, then he reached deep into the truck's bed and took hold of something heavy. Straightening himself with a forceful grunt, he began to pull the carcass of an eight-point buck into view when the cabin door suddenly burst wide open.

A hawk-faced man with shoulder-length silver-blonde hair stood in the doorway. His expression an ugly rage. *"Get off my land!"* he howled. *"You got no right to be here!"*

Pierce slid the bloody carcass from the truck and let it drop to the ground in an ungraceful, flopping heap. Then he turned toward the man. His gaze level, penetrating. "State Game Commission," he said. "Is this your deer?"

"That's right!" Gunner returned sharply. "Now get off my property!"

Pierce pressed his lips into a thin line. "I have a few questions, first." He nodded toward the second deer. "Who killed the doe?"

Although the trooper was in plain view, a mere 10 yards away, Gunner never noticed him. For his focus — his utter contempt, his loathing — remained totally on the deputy. He stood in his open doorway for what seemed an eternity, glaring at Pierce in an awkward attempt to stare him down. The two men, with their stony gunslinger faces, reminded the trooper of Clint Eastwood and Lee Van Cleef facing each other in a Mexican standoff during the final minutes of Sergio Leone's epic western, *The Good, the Bad and the Ugly*. And indeed, the steely-eyed Gunner even bore an uncanny resemblance to the villainous bounty hunter played by Van Cleef.

But unlike Van Cleef, who stood ramrod straight until Eastwood gunned him down, Gunner looked a bit tipsy and quickly threw a hand against the doorjamb for support. His menacing stare melted into a look of genuine surprise. "Deer season opened today," he said. "Man's not allowed to hunt on his own land?"

"Not when it's baited," said Pierce.

Gunner looked insulted. He pointed a crooked finger at the deputy and waggled it. "Wait just a minute mister," he said. "Those deer are both legal kills."

"Then I guess you won't mind if my partner and I ask you a few questions."

Partner...? Gunner blinked stupidly and glanced around. He spied the young trooper standing within spitting distance. *Yes . . . there had been two of them!* "I see you brought the cavalry along!"

"No, the cavalry is just over the hill," Pierce said mockingly. "There's just the two of us here."

Gunner pushed himself off the doorjamb and snorted at the deputy. "Like I said, the deer are both legal. I got the buck. Fred killed the doe." He turned and hollered into the cabin. "Fred! Come on out here!"

Soon a chubby balding man in his late fifties sauntered to the door scratching his bewhiskered face absently. "Game wardens!" he gasped in feigned surprise. "Have we done something wrong?"

Pierce recognized him instantly. He was the same man who had been sitting next to Gunner in court when Judge Vanston became annoyed by their antics. And he remembered Wasserman's comment regarding the two of them: *Every dog has his day!* he had said. But there had been doubt in the warden's voice.

Pierce realized full well that most poachers got away with their unlawful hunting activities because game wardens simply covered too much territory to apprehend them effectively. Wasserman often joked that his district covered 400 square miles — but that didn't count going up and down the mountains. It was a lot of territory to be sure. The chances of coming across a poacher in the act were slim at best. Too many of them killed with impunity, never to be brought to justice. But Pierce was determined not to let that happen today.

"I want to see two hunting licenses," he said. His voice clearly indicating that he intended calling the shots from this point forward.

Fred glanced nervously at the trooper and back to the deputy. "Sure thing, officer," he said. "Why don't you and your associate step inside. I'll get them for you."

Gunner gawked in wide-eyed disbelief as Pierce brushed past him and motioned the trooper to follow him into the cabin. Jesse strode to the porch and stopped in front of Gunner. "After you," he said.

Spartan by design, the log building was divided by a single wall, with one section for sleeping while the other served as a combined kitchen and living area. Two well-worn stuffed chairs, a shabby old couch, and a faded wooden card table decorated the living room, while the kitchen consisted of a few cheap, metal storage cabinets and a stainless steel sink surrounded by a Formica countertop. Cases of beer were piled against the walls like pillars in a coliseum, their remnant empty bottles strewn helter-skelter about the cabin floor.

Fred lifted two hunting licenses off the kitchen counter and handed them to Pierce. The deputy took them, pulled a notebook from his coat pocket, and copied down the information he needed for his citations. Fred stared anxiously at the deputy as he wrote. "Are we in some kind of trouble?" he asked.

"Depends," said Pierce, knowing they were in all the trouble he could possibly find for them. "Where'd you kill the deer?"

"Behind the cabin. Gut piles are still there if you want to see 'em."

Pierce stuffed his notebook back into his pocket and nodded. "Yeah, I would." Turning to Jesse, he said, "Mind keeping Mr. Gunner company while Fred and I take a little walk?"

The trooper glanced at Gunner. He was sitting in a chair, elbows on knees, hands clasped against both sides of his head as if trying to keep his brains from exploding into the room. "No problem," Jesse said.

When Pierce walked behind the cabin, he found a 50-pound salt block and a bushel of grocery-fresh apples dumped directly below the balcony. Deer tracks and droppings were mingled with the bait; and much of it had been worked over by them, as well as turkeys and other critters. Pierce pulled a camera from his back pocket and glanced at Fred, whose face revealed an expression of relief that the matter was coming to a close.

After photographing the bait, Pierce walked over to the two gut piles he saw lying nearby. He pulled a small hunting knife from his belt sheath and cut the stomachs open on both of them. They consisted entirely of undigested apples. It was obvious that the deer had been lured to the bait and then shot right from the balcony of Gunner's cabin. Pierce photographed the gut piles and then pocketed his camera. "I've seen enough," he said soberly. "Let's head back inside."

When they stepped into the cabin, Gunner looked up from his chair, muttered something foul under his breath, and glowered at Fred for ratting them out. Pierce shook his head in pathetic disbelief. The bait under the balcony had been in plain view, he could have found it blindfolded. But poor Fred, unable to face his partner, dropped his anxious eyes and pointed his nose at the floor.

Fred's submissive posture only served to enrage Joe Gunner. Leaping from his chair, he launched into a thunderous tirade about the Gestapo tactics used by game wardens and how they were constantly trespassing on private property and persecuting honest hunters.

"AND YOU!" he roared at the trooper, his face an ugly scowl. *"YOU'RE A STATE COP! YOU SHOULD KNOW BETTER YOU ROTTEN BAHHhhhh . . .!"*

Gunner's last word died in his throat, his mouth agape as he stared at the nametag pinned to the trooper's chest. Upon it the inscription of a surname that he recognized instantly.

Pierce, who'd been waiting all day for this very moment, broke into a roguish grin as the trooper began to dress down the man he'd miraculously turned to stone: "You might own the land, Mr. Gunner," he said as he came nose to nose with him, "but that doesn't give you the right to kill game illegally or to interfere with a lawful investigation. Now I'm giving you two choices: You can be civil and stay right here in your snug little cabin, or you can keep mouthing off and come with us in cuffs. It's up to you."

The poacher remained silent for a moment, his hardened eyes peering warily at the trooper. Then, finally, calculatingly, he spoke: "Wasserman!" he hissed in a low, cold voice. "The game warden! He must be your old man. You act just like him."

"I'll take that as a complement," the trooper replied. "Now simmer down so we can finish up and get out of here."

Gunner raised both palms defensively. "No problem. I'll back off. But you can't take our deer!" He turned toward Pierce. "You can't," he said with an emphatic whine. "They're both tagged and legal."

"Legal!" scoffed Pierce. "How do you figure that?"

"We didn't put the apples and salt out back until after we killed them," insisted Gunner. "We just wanted to feed the animals now that we've filled our tags, that's all."

Pierce shook his head wearily. "Nice try," he said, "but I got a tip that your camp was baited a week ago and stopped in for a look when nobody was around. Saw the same salt and apples then that are here today." He paused, his eyes studying the solemn faces of both men. "I think you two have been at this game for years; you just happened to get caught this time. Citations will be coming in the mail. You're each looking at a $1000 fine plus three years loss of your hunting privileges. Now, my partner and I have wasted enough time here today. Got anything else to say — say it to a judge."

As the deputy's pickup truck cruised down the narrow country road with its contraband, two uniformed men sat side by side and reminisced about days gone by: For the deputy, they were days filled with glory and adventure pursuing poachers across the rugged mountains of northern Pennsylvania. But the trooper's thoughts were of a different nature, and his face exuded a dreamy, melancholy appearance.

The deputy looked at him and frowned, for he knew him well. "Heard from your father lately?" he asked.

The trooper shifted his weight and gazed wistfully at the countryside streaming by. "Yes," he said with a fading smile. "We call each other almost every day."

The deputy nodded. "That's good," he said glancing at the trooper and then back to the road again. "He'll be pleased to hear that we arrested Joe Gunner."

The trooper chuckled softly. "Yeah. He sure will."

The deputy looked again at the young man sitting next to him, and a lifetime of memories flashed through his mind in a millisecond. "Sure wish he hadn't retired and moved south," he said.

"Me too," said the trooper.

"By the way, you hungry?"

"Starved!"

"New donut shop in town," the deputy said suggestively.

"So I hear!" replied the trooper with a wry smile. "But I was thinking steak and eggs."

The deputy let out a bark of laughter and slapped his knee with a calloused hand. "I knew you'd say that!" he roared in sunny delight. "Sounds wonderful! I think I'll have the same — and I'm buying, it's the least I can do after you came along to back me up today."

"Fair enough," replied the trooper. "And since we're talking chow, what about the two deer in the back?"

"I keep a list of needy families, Jesse. They'll be put to good use, believe me."

The trooper leaned back into his seat and nodded contentedly. "Excellent!" he said. "I love a happy ending."

"Yes," the deputy replied with a broad smile. "A happy ending indeed."

Fasten your seatbelts. It's going to be a bumpy night.
— Joseph Leo Mankiewicz

Hawkeye

ZIGGY **AND JED** had been cruising the back roads in their rundown pickup truck for hours when they finally spotted the buck. A spectacular eight-pointer, it stood before them in the grassy field like a great bronze statue, its massive head high in the air.

"Man, look at that!" crowed Jed, his foot nudging the brake peddle. He peered into his rearview mirror. Behind him, the desolate country road stretched for a half-mile then disappeared around a wooded bend. "No one's around, Zig, you could hit him easy from right here!"

Ziggy whipped his head toward his brother. "Keep driving!" he barked. "You're gonna spook him!"

Jed winced under his brother's sharp rebuke and stepped on the accelerator. Ziggy had a quick temper, and Jed, knowing better than to back talk him, drove on in glum silence. But he had only traveled a short distance when he found his voice again: "There's a bend just ahead!" he exclaimed. "Once we get around the corner I'll pull over and you can jump in the back." He glanced timidly at his brother. "Okay, Zig?"

Ziggy nodded in silent agreement. The buck would be an easy target but they would have to be quick about it. Someone might come along and see them at any second.

As soon as Jed rounded the bend, he came to a lurching stop, his knuckles white on the steering wheel. Ziggy didn't waste a second. Jerking open the door, he sprinted to the back of the truck with his bow and dropped it into the bed. Then he clambered over the tailgate, sank into a low squat, and grabbed the side rail with both hands. "Go! Go! Go!" he hollered,

Jed wheeled his truck around and drove back toward the deer, his eyes darting nervously into the rearview mirror as he sped down the road. Soon he could see the animal grazing in the distant field, the low sun reflecting off its huge porcelain-like antlers as he drew near. His heart pounding wildly, he inched alongside the doomed whitetail and eased on the brake. But as he pulled broadside to the deer a scatter of gravel crackled like popcorn under his tires, causing the regal buck to lift his head in mild curiosity.

Dressed in full camouflage, Ziggy remained low against the tailgate with his head down until the truck came to a complete stop. Then, like morning fog rising from a pond, he stood and drew his bow in one fluid motion, bringing his string hand to the corner of his chin. By the time the deer sensed danger, Ziggy had already relaxed his fingers, his fatal missile searing the air.

When the broadhead struck, the frantic whitetail leaped high into the air and bolted toward the distant tree line. But the arrow had bored deep into its side, and though the deer ran strong and hard, it soon began to weaken as blood streamed from a severed artery. In less than a minute its front knees suddenly buckled, causing the deer to pitch headfirst into the ground and then flip hooves-over-antlers into a floundering summersault before collapsing.

Jed slapped his knees and let out a bloodcurdling howl as he watched the trophy buck fall at the woods edge. His brother never missed — and this had been no exception. Pulling himself halfway out the truck's window, he twisted his body toward the tailgate and shoved a jubilant thumb into the air. *"HOOOOOAHHH!"* he bellowed.

Ziggy smiled back at him, leaped athletically to the ground, and ran to the front of the truck. "Did you see that sucker jump!" he chuckled, yanking open the passenger door.

Jed looked at him and smiled. *"Hawkeye!"* he breathed as Ziggy pitched his bow inside the cab.

Ziggy threw his head back and let out a great, belly laugh. His brother always made him laugh when he called him that. And Jed would only do it when they were poaching deer together. "You're right!" Ziggy crowed. "It *was* a great shot!" Then he glanced over his shoulder at the road behind them and turned back to his brother. "Now get the heck out of here before someone sees us!"

Jed dropped his truck into gear and sped off while Ziggy made a 100-yard dash to the deer. As soon as he reached the carcass, he dropped to his knees and glanced back at the road. Jed was long gone. He listened for an approaching vehicle in the distance, a hunter or the landowner perhaps, but only heard the soft autumn breeze blowing lazily through the trees behind him. Satisfied that no one was coming, Ziggy pulled his hunting knife from its leather sheath and opened the deer from belly to sternum with a single thrust. In seconds, the entrails were removed and dropped into a steaming pile alongside the carcass. Ziggy took the deer by its antlers and quickly dragged the carcass out of sight into the woods. Breathing heavily, he glanced at his watch. It would be dark in one hour.

Filled with a glowing sense of satisfaction, Ziggy sat next to a huge oak tree and cradled his back against its rough bark to await his brother's return. He could relax now. No one could see him here. And as the heavy, sweet scent of autumn leaves filled his nostrils, he grabbed a pack of cigarettes from his shirt pocket and lit up a fresh smoke. It had been a very good day, he thought. Yes, a very good day indeed.

In what seemed like mere seconds, the guttural rumble of an approaching vehicle jolted him awake. There was only darkness now. Darkness and the ascending steady drone of a vehicle drawing near. Ziggy crouched by the tree and peered into the night, eyes straining to see. Whoever was coming had their headlights turned off, and the grim notion that it might be the game warden caused his scalp to grow tight.

He heard the harsh squeal of a braking vehicle, then an engine idling roughly. The vehicle had stopped directly ahead of him at the field's edge, but the moonless night made it impossible to see who it was. Then the engine went dead and he heard the grating creak of a neglected door slowly opening.

Someone was coming!

Ziggy's heart began to race; he could hear it pounding in his head. He rubbed his eyes and refocused, attempting in vain to see who was there. He stood, ready to flee, his chest tightening into an agonizing knot. Then —

"HAWWWKEYEEEE!"

The call came to him like a song in the night.

It was Jed! Jed, thank goodness!

Ziggy grabbed the deer by its heavy antlers and cupped a hand to his mouth. "Comin' at ya!" he cried.

Jed had known better than to drive his truck into the field for the deer. It would be a dead giveaway if anyone spotted him. So he stayed by the road and watched for approaching headlights as Ziggy brought the deer to him. If anyone came along, he would jump in his truck and take off while Ziggy flattened himself in the long grass and waited for the vehicle to pass.

But the night remained tranquil, the road vacant. And Ziggy's lean body soon emerged from the murky field, breathless from his hard work. Jed unlatched his rusty tailgate and let it drop on its hinges with a resounding clang. Then, after helping Ziggy heave the carcass into the truck's bed, he slammed the tailgate shut and raced his brother to the front seat, jumping in alongside him. The brothers stared at each other for a moment, then Ziggy bellowed a triumphant warrior's whoop and the young men smacked hands. *"Hawkeye!"* Jed whispered shaking his head in feigned reverence. And with that, both men began to laugh hysterically as they sped into the night.

When Jed turned off the main highway and started down the road leading to their house, Ziggy whipped his head toward his brother and frowned. "Where are *you* going?"

"Home. Why?"

"We can't go home! Bow season doesn't open until tomorrow; somebody will see the deer!"

"What else can we do, Zig? I'll get a tarp and cover it. Nobody's gonna see anything."

"No way! Can't risk it. We'll take the deer a little further up the road and hide it in the woods. Then I'll come back tomorrow morning and tag it." Ziggy snapped his fingers. "Presto! The deer suddenly becomes legal."

Jed looked bewildered. "But Wasserman lives on the other side of the woods! What if he sees us?"

"The old man is probably snoring on his couch already," Ziggy scoffed. "Look, just stop up ahead and I'll jump out and drag the deer into the brush while you head home. Then I'll cut through the woods and meet you at the house later."

Jed nodded in loyal obedience and soon found himself pulling to the berm while Ziggy leaped out the passenger door and ran to the back. He dropped the tailgate, grabbed the buck by its antlers, and gave the deer a fierce tug. The trophy whitetail slid from the bed and hit the ground with a thud. Then Ziggy waved his brother on and quickly made off with his prize.

But in his haste to drag the carcass out of sight and into the woods, he ran blindly into a vast Greenbrier thicket. The prickly thorns enveloped him like a giant web, stapling themselves to his legs, chest, and face. Ziggy yowled in agony as he peeled the tortuous barbs from his bloodied skin and backed away. He had stupidly allowed his brother to drop him off in front of an impenetrable barrier of thorns!

The miscalculation had kept him too close to the road for too long. Anyone could come along and see him. He ran with the deer now, dragging the carcass frantically alongside the briers for what seemed an eternity until finally coming to an opening: an ATV trail that broke from the woods directly onto the roadway.

Exhausted from dragging the heavy carcass so far, Ziggy pulled it a short distance into the trail and hid it behind a large rotted log for safekeeping until morning. Then, instead of heading home like he'd promised his brother, he turned in the opposite direction and walked out of the woods into a grassy meadow high on a hill. Here he sat on a large flat rock, gazed into the cool starry distance, and lit up a fresh Marlboro.

Ziggy took a leisurely pull on his cigarette and stared down at the cluster of homes nestled in the tiny valley a quarter mile away. He could see the warden's house from his lofty perch, and he chuckled softly. The kitchen light was on.

He was probably having dinner with his family right now, wondering about how many hunters he'd be arresting tomorrow. Ziggy wasn't worried, though. He had fooled him before and he would do it again. And this time it would be extra sweet because the deer was hidden practically under the warden's nose. Wasserman, as always, would leave at the crack of dawn to begin his patrol. All Ziggy needed to do was give him some time to get out of the area before he returned to retrieve his deer.

Ziggy took another drag on his cigarette and let the smoke escape slowly through his nostrils as he thought back on his previous run-in with the warden.

It had been little more than a year ago, not far from where he sat at this very moment, as a matter of fact. He had taken a shot at a dove. Missed it clean too. Then, from out of nowhere, a game warden was standing opposite him at the far end of the pines, straight as a danged statue. Just like he'd popped out of the ground or something. Badge all shiny in the sunshine even from the hundred yards that separated the two of them.

Ziggy couldn't make out the face but reckoned it had to be Wasserman; he was hunting within view of the warden's house. Small game season was open. Why wasn't the man out patrolling the county, anyway? He glanced at his watch: Noon. Lunchtime. Wasserman probably spotted him right from his kitchen window, his bright orange vest a dead giveaway in the blazing sun. Stupid! Stupid. Stupid. Never should have taken that shot!

Ziggy bolted.

He ran as fast as his young legs would carry him. Nimbly he passed over the rough and broken terrain. Leaping across a narrow brook like an Olympic long jumper, he charged frantically across an open meadow and disappeared into a dense grove of evergreens. He dropped to the ground, heart pounding wildly against his ribs, and then quickly flipped his jacket inside out to display the mottled green-and-brown camouflage that would match the trousers he wore. Zipping up, he flattened himself on the frigid ground and became all but invisible from a distance. Then, with his camouflage hood covering his head, Ziggy lifted his chin to steal a look down the long column of silky trees.

There! He saw him go by in a fleeting instant. Running at the far end of the grove, glancing into each open row as he passed. Pursuing an orange vest, he had looked right at Ziggy and missed him. Safe for now, he continued to lay stock-still and waited for the warden to abandon his search.

That is, until he had to pee.

Lying on his belly on the cold October ground had caused a chill to work its way deep into his loins, and his body began to ache with a painful urgency. He listened for something that would indicate where the game warden might be lurking: A muffled cough or a sniffle — the snap of a twig, perhaps.

Something.

Anything!

Instead, he heard only the sound of his own shallow breathing amid the whispering pines.

His need unbearable, he slowly pulled himself up and stood. But before he could relieve himself, a voice drifted through the trees and he froze.

"Five-three-eight to any deputy . . . "

Ziggy tilted his head slowly upward and peered through the bluish-green pine needles concealing his face. There, three rows away, stood Wasserman with his back to him, his portable radio held to his face. The warden was calling for backup! Soon his deputies would appear. And they'd be searching for him row by row.

Melting slowly downward into a squat, Ziggy calculated his next move. It was obvious that the warden hadn't seen him. But if he didn't make a break for it now, he'd soon be discovered. He had no choice. He had to take his chances and get out of there!

Slithering on his belly, shotgun slung over his shoulder, Ziggy edged silently down the long row of pines until he reached the end. Here a meadow the length of a football field spilled into a dense woodlot. If he could get to the woods without being seen, he'd be safe. His house lay just on the other side of the trees. Standing now, Ziggy glanced back over his shoulder, and, seeing it was all clear, he dashed across the meadow and into the woods.

Ziggy ran through the trees in a wild panic until he finally reached his house. Crashing through the front door, he barely looked at his mother as she turned in sudden bewilderment from the kitchen table. *"Ziggy!"* she cried. *"Land sakes, are you —* "

"Gotta go, Ma! Gotta go!" he howled as he dashed down the long hallway toward the open bathroom door . . .

Ziggy smiled as he recalled the expression of open surprise on his mother's face that day. Then he stood, crushed his Marlboro under the toe of his leather boot, and took one last look at the warden's house. "Guess the old man is losing his touch," he muttered under his breath. And with that, he turned and sprinted through the deep dark woods toward his home.

I NEVER EXPECTED to run into Ziggy that fateful morning — and had I not been delayed by an urgent, albeit long-winded phone conversation, I would have missed him. But as I drove along the state highway that bordered my neighborhood, I happened to glance into the woods on my right and saw a hunter dressed in camouflage crouching over a large buck. He looked up and spotted me at the same moment, and his arms and legs started flailing about in a dozen different directions at once. Then suddenly he was on his feet, running frantically toward his four-wheeler.

I jammed my brakes and threw my Ford Expedition into reverse. *He'll be gone in seconds*, I thought as I launched forward through a narrow opening into the woods. Directly in front of me now, he was running along an ATV trail, his head down so I couldn't see his face as I came at him.

Leaping on his machine cowboy style, he started the engine and wrenched back on the hand-throttle, his knobby tires digging furiously into the earth. Because the four-wheeler faced toward me, I quickly slammed my brakes thinking surely we'd crash once his tires took hold. But as they did, he lifted himself off the seat and shifted his body left while simultaneously turning the handlebar. Then, spinning into an abrupt U-turn, he sent a raging hailstorm of dirt and debris into my windshield as he fled down the narrow ATV trail.

I shadowed him, my cumbersome Expedition barely squeezing by the trees on either side. I was acting on pure adrenaline now, knowing the chase couldn't last. Unless his machine broke down or ran out of gas, I'd never catch him. The trail was extremely rough, and the bleak notion that I might tear out my undercarriage at any given moment loomed in my mind. Suddenly an uninviting knoll reared just ahead. I decked the brakes, tires sliding across rotting leaves as I watched the fleeing ATV catapult into the air and vanish before my eyes.

My shoulder harness slammed into my chest as I skidded to a dead stop over the knoll. The wheelbase too long, my truck had hung up. I shoved open the door and leaped out. In the distance, I could hear the rough mechanical thrum of an ATV fading into oblivion.

Leaving my patrol car seesawing on the knoll, rear tires spinning absurdly in the air, I took off on foot hoping he might bog down somewhere. I sprinted along the broken terrain as fast as I could, considering my bulky uniform, the narrow trail twisting and turning as I pushed ahead. After running a hundred yards, I came to a crossroad on my left and stopped. The acrid smell of exhaust fumes hung heavily in the air here, revealing that he had slowed down to make a turn and then accelerated hard once again. Through the trees, I could see a sizeable housing development in the distance. The road led directly to it.

All at once, I noticed the sun glinting off an object on the trail just ahead. Curious, I walked over for a closer look and was surprised to see a plastic hunting license holder with the license still inside. It must have come from the four-wheeler I'd been chasing. Stooping down, my pulse quickened as I pulled the cardboard certificate from its plastic sheath and read the owner's name: Siegfried Zagg.

Tapping the license contemplatively against its plastic holder, I recalled the incident at the Christmas tree farm last year. Ziggy had vanished in thin air that day just like he had today. He had gotten away from me once but it wasn't going to happen again. And with that thought in mind, I jogged quickly back to my embedded vehicle.

After taking a good look under the frame, I breathed a sigh of relief when I saw there was no damage to the undercarriage. I had been stuck more times than I could count over the years, and in far worse places. With some support under the drive wheels, I would be home free in no time.

I quickly scrounged up a dozen good-sized rocks and a couple of logs, and jammed them under my wheels. Climbing inside the vehicle, I dropped it into reverse and pressed gently against the gas peddle. I felt my tires grab hold of the makeshift base, and smiled optimistically as I began to inch the long-bodied Expedition off the knoll.

After leveling out, I continued to back the cumbersome Ford along the trail, wondering why the agency had ever decided to go with such an unwieldy vehicle for game wardens to patrol in. While superb on the highway and impressive to look at, the long wheelbase proved to be problematic whenever I took it off-road, which, in my case, was more often than I should have.

When I finally backed into the clearing where Ziggy had abandoned his eight-pointer, I was surprised to see Deputy Gaydos kneeling by the carcass. He stood and walked over to my vehicle.

"What brought *you* here?" I asked stepping out the door to grab his palm. Deputy Gene Gaydos — with 35-years service — was one of only a few field officers still on the job that had more time on than I did. And he was a crack investigator.

Gaydos cocked his head toward the deer. "I was driving by when I looked over and saw the buck lying there. Didn't seem right, so I thought I'd better check it out." He peered critically at my patrol car: A tortured branch poked from the undercarriage like a long bony arm; the windshield and fenders covered with dirt from Ziggy's wild escape. "Good thing too," he added with a mischievous twinkle in his eye, "it looks like you need some help!"

"Story of my life," I grinned in agreement. "The poacher must have thought so too. He left this behind." I handed Ziggy's license to my deputy and watched his jaw slowly come unhinged as he examined the name. "I was just on my way to pay the young man a visit, find out why he ran."

Gaydos looked up at me and frowned. "The deer was killed yesterday. I think that would be reason enough, don't you?"

"Say what!"

"You didn't know?"

I nodded at my patrol car. "Pretty tough to tell when you're traveling at warp speed."

Gaydos chuckled at the notion. Then he turned toward the deer and put his hands on his hips. "Eyes are glazed. Rigor mortis too — stiff as a board! I measured the body heat while you were back there chasing after Ziggy. My thermometer says the deer was killed less than 24 hours ago."

I looked at the heavily antlered buck for a long moment. "Would have made a dandy trophy for somebody."

Gaydos nodded in solemn agreement. "Poachers!" he grunted. "No better than common thieves."

After securing the deer to my big game carrier, Gaydos and I drove to the housing development bordering the woods. It was Saturday, school was out, and most folks were home from work while their children played in the narrow streets. All heads turned as we motored by, their necks craning to catch a glimpse of the giant buck we had in tow.

I stopped in front of Ziggy's place and noticed a battered pickup truck parked in the driveway. "Somebody must be home," I said as we walked past.

Gaydos glanced at the truck, then looked at me with a raised brow. "Did you see the blood?"

I looked again, concealing my surprise, for I had missed it. There was a small crimson stain running along the white bumper. "Wondered how long it would take you to notice that," I said dryly.

Gaydos gave me a questioning side-glance and I quickly rapped on the door as he opened his mouth to comment.

"Just a minute!" boomed a woman's voice from inside. I heard the scrape of a chair pulling back, and then heavy footsteps approaching. Ziggy's mother opened the door and eyed us suspiciously for a moment, her ample body crowding the doorway. "Game Wardens!" she sighed wearily. "What did he do now?"

Gaydos and I were in full uniform. I told her we suspected that Ziggy had killed a deer unlawfully and that we wanted to talk to him about it.

The woman put both fists on her broad hips and looked toward the back of the house. *"SIEEEGFRIEEEED! GET OUT HERE RIGHT NOW!"*

She smiled at us sheepishly, her voice softening. "Lordy," she said, "where are my manners? Please, come in gentlemen."

We stepped into the modest home and stood on a tattered rug in the living room while waiting for Ziggy to appear. There was a long narrow hallway to our left that led back to the bedrooms and bath. To our immediate right, a cramped kitchen, its worn Formica counter heaped with unwashed frying pans and dishes encrusted with food.

Ziggy's mother saw me glance into the kitchen. "It's a mess," she said with a blushing grin. "I was just about to clean up before work this morning."

"I'm sure you weren't expecting company, ma'am," I said. "Sorry about the intrusion."

She nodded softly and brushed a long straggle of hair from her face. "Coffee?"

"No thanks, ma'am. Your son . . . he *is* here, isn't he?"

"Ziggy works night shift," his mother politely explained. "He's probably getting some clothes on. Just be a minute."

And it was at that very moment that Ziggy came shuffling down the hallway from a back room. He was shadowed by a pregnant teenaged girl. Tall and lanky, with a generous mop of uncombed strawberry-blonde hair, he wore a pair of faded blue jeans and a white T-shirt. Ziggy's eyes locked on the badge pinned to my chest and his face turned ashen. "I shouldn't have run," he sighed. "I knew I shouldn't have run."

"That's not all you shouldn't have done," I leveled at him. "We know your deer was killed yesterday, not today."

Ziggy cocked his head and tried to look surprised. "Not *my* deer! I killed it this morning. Honest!"

"Then why did you run when you saw me?"

"I was scared 'cause I killed it on private property."

"Where on private property?"

"Across the road from where you first saw me with the deer."

I glanced at his mother, her grim eyes searching nervously from her son back to me as I questioned him.

"Where across the road?" I pressed.

"Back in the Christmas tree farm," he replied. And the ghost of a smile crossed his lips.

Deputy Gaydos suddenly broke in: "Son," he said firmly, "I've been hunting deer for more than 50 years. Killed more big bucks than you've got years on this earth. I don't care what you say or how you say it, that deer wasn't killed this morning."

"Honest!" Ziggy cried. "And I would have tagged it too, until I saw *him* come flying into the woods in his police car." He was pointing an accusatory finger directly at me. "I was scared, that's all. I ain't done nothing wrong!"

Although certain the deer had been killed before the season opened, neither Gaydos nor I possessed any kind of scientific degree in time-of-death analysis. If Ziggy stuck with his story and we ended up in court, there was a good chance we would lose the case.

What I needed was a good old-fashioned confession, but it didn't look too promising. Ziggy was bent on sticking with his story. It almost seemed like he was enjoying himself while Gaydos and I tried to crack him.

Suddenly I remembered the pickup truck parked outside. What if it wasn't his? What if someone had helped him transport the deer? Someone more talkative, perhaps.

"Who owns the truck out back?" I asked his mother. "There's blood on the back bumper."

Upon hearing the question, Ziggy's mother looked like she was about to faint. She grabbed the back of a chair for support and shook her head miserably. Ziggy watched her, and his face began to wrinkle with concern. "It's my brother's truck," he mumbled at the floor. "My brother Jed."

"Where can I find him?" I said.

Ziggy shrugged his shoulders, telling me he had no idea. His mother folded her arms across her chest and glared at him with disapproval. She turned to me. "He's here," she said. "Probably hiding under his bed!"

"I'd like to speak with him."

"And so would I." Ziggy's mother turned toward the long hallway, cupped a hand to the side of her mouth, and called her son. *JEDEDIAAAH! YOU BETTER COME OUT HERE RIGHT NOW!*

From a back bedroom came Jedediah Zagg. He shambled down the narrow hallway and stood before us white-faced with fear. He glanced at his brother and then stared at his mother questioningly for a moment before turning to me. "What's this all about?"

I looked at his mother, suspecting that her domineering presence would work in my favor, and waited.

Her face flushed with rage, she scolded her sons. "You two have brought shame and embarrassment to my house. You might think you're fooling these officers, but believe me you're not! They know exactly what you did; you're just making things worse by lying to them." Her eyes brimming with tears, she put her hands on her hips and leaned into her sons. "This is my house! If you want to continue living here, you better start telling the truth. *And I mean right now!*"

The brothers eyed each other briefly, then Ziggy nodded submissively at Jed, indicating it was time to throw in the towel. They turned to face me.

"You got us," admitted Ziggy with a thin shrug of despair. "I killed the buck yesterday afternoon about five miles from here. Shot it with my bow from the bed of Jed's truck. Then we hid it until this morning when you caught me." He ran a hand through his thick, unruly hair, and looked at me angrily. "Satisfied?"

I shook my head. "Not enough, Ziggy. I want you to tell me every detail about what you and your brother did. I want to know the who, when, what, where, and why about the deer. I want to know it step-by-step and minute-by-minute. Everything. Understood?"

Ziggy stiffened. "Yes, sir."

"And when you're finished, we're going to have a discussion about the incident at the Christmas tree farm last fall."

Ziggy gulped hard, his eyes shifting from his mother back to me. "What incident . . . ?"

"Siegfrieeed!" his mother said acidly. "Don't you dare lie to this man."

Ziggy looked at his mother and flinched painfully. "Yes ma'am." Turning to me he said, "C'mon, we'll sit at the kitchen table and get this over with. I'll tell you everything you want to know."

When Ziggy finished his confession I was tempted to throw the book at him and Jed both, which would have brought their fines soaring to well over $2000, but his mother persuaded me to reconsider. Her eyes moist and pleading, she explained that Ziggy was only earning minimum wage, and that he and his pregnant girlfriend were living with her so she could help them get a decent start in life. She added that Jed lived there too, and lent a hand with the bills, but only had a part-time job.

My eyes moved from Ziggy's tearful mother to the wide-eyed and pregnant teenaged girl she had pulled close to her bosom, and I felt my animosity toward the young men begin to slowly evaporate. I thought about the difficult situation the entire family was facing, and realized that multiple charges against the two poachers would have punished everyone in the household. I didn't want to do that. Thus, I wrote one single citation for both Ziggy and his brother. Each carried a $500 fine and included revocation of their hunting and trapping privileges for three consecutive years. The minimum for unlawfully killing a deer.

Both Jed and Ziggy pled guilty in court and were put on time-payments until their fines were paid off. Jed managed to find a full-time job and has stayed out of trouble ever since. Unfortunately, I can't say the same about Ziggy. For a chance encounter brought us face-to-face once again. But that, my friends, remains a story for another day.

If all men were just, there would be no need of valor.
— Agesilaus
444 - 400 B.C.

Butch Striker

WHEN THE PHONE rang, Deputy Gene Gaydos didn't know he was about to have a run-in with Butch Striker. The informant never mentioned any names, including his own, when he reported two deer poachers. "Just head over to Tamarack Road," he said in a low voice. "There's a trail that cuts into the woods by a red barn. They'll come out that way."

Then the line went dead.

His wife watched him hang up the receiver and knew instantly that his dinner would have to wait. She could read him like a book. "I'll put it back in the oven," she said, "keep it warm till you get back." She'd lost count long ago of the interrupted meals and middle-of-the-night phone calls her husband had endured over the years.

"Thanks, Judy," he said. "I shouldn't be too long."

She forced a smile, knowing full well that he could be gone all night. And that would be okay, as long as he came back safely.

"Be careful," she called as she opened the oven and slid his plate inside.

But he was already out the door.

No sooner had the deputy pulled in by the red barn when a rifle shot echoed through the woods. It sounded about a hundred yards off, so he quickly blocked the trail with his pickup truck and waited for the hunters to appear.

A half hour passed, and darkness was setting in when Gaydos suddenly heard the low staccato hum of an ATV in the distance. It was coming his way — and it was moving fast! He quickly exited his vehicle and placed himself several yards down the trail to intercept it.

Within seconds, the machine scudded around a bend and came to a jarring stop in front of him. Two hunters dressed in camouflage, their rifles in leather side-cases, sat astride a muddy four-wheeler and stared at the uniformed deputy in surprise. The trail, bordered by dense brush, was too narrow for them to turn around, and it looked like he had them cold. But as he strode toward his suspects, the machine suddenly came hurtling right at him.

"State officer!" he cried with a raised palm. "Halt!"

His life flashed before his eyes as the machine slammed to a stop mere inches away, its hellish engine revving menacingly. Gaydos could see the operator plainly now, his eyes blazing with hatred for the daring lawman. A passenger sat close behind him, face buried between his shoulders, unidentifiable.

"Shut down the engine, now!" the deputy commanded.

Instead, the driver cut his wheels and whipped the four-wheeler sharply around Gaydos, missing him by a hair as he veered into the darkening woods. Desperate, the outlaw fled through the forest at a remarkable pace, weaving around deadly trees with the agility of a slalom skiing ace.

Gaydos raced toward his truck as the machine's rough whine faded into the gloom. He could hear the direction it was heading, and hoped he might overtake it, when the motor suddenly died.

He's home! the deputy thought with fixed determination, *and he can't be far!*

Jumping into his truck, he backed out of the trail and started down the road in the direction the suspects had fled. He soon came to a long row of modest homes on his right, and slowed to a crawl hoping to see the four-wheeler parked nearby, when he spotted a man working under the hood of a car in his driveway. Gaydos stopped along the road and walked over to him.

"State game warden, sir. An ATV just came this way. Have you seen it?"

The man looked over his shoulder, raised one long finger to his lips, and then pointed to his neighbor's property. He quickly ducked back under the hood. "Please! Go away! I don't want him to see you here. He's trouble!"

The deputy turned in the direction indicated. There, one house over in a back yard hidden from the roadway, he saw the four-wheeler.

Gaydos walked to the house and knocked on a glass storm door that led directly into a well-lit kitchen. Inside, he could see a heavy elderly woman and her male companion sitting at a table like statues in a wax museum. The woman's back was toward him while her male companion sat opposite her and studied the floor. Between them stood a small boy in cotton pajamas, his questioning eyes dancing to and fro at the frozen grown-ups. "Grammy," he pointed, "there's a policeman at the door!" His little lips formed a pink circle of surprise as he stared wide-eyed at the officer.

Again, Gaydos knocked, louder this time, and the boy began to tug frantically at his grandmother's fleshy arm. "Grammy, Grammy, there's a policeman at the door. A policeman, Grammy!" And had the child not been so hopelessly persistent the woman may never have budged.

"Whadaya want?" she hollered over her shoulder.

"State game warden, ma'am. Would you come to the door please?"

Straining to her feet, the woman lumbered to the door and peered at him through the glass barrier. "Well . . . ?"

"Would you mind opening the door?" said Gaydos. "I'd like to talk to you for a moment."

The woman glanced down at the child, scolding him with her eyes for speaking out as she reached for the door. It creaked partially open. "What do you want?"

Gaydos nodded at the four-wheeler. "Where's the driver of the ATV?"

"That thing!" the old woman scoffed. "Nobody's driven it for weeks. It don't even run no more!"

"Afraid not, ma'am," frowned Gaydos. "The engine is still warm. Somebody just parked it."

The woman pressed her lips tightly as Gaydos continued: "He had long red hair, kind of tall, camouflage clothes . . . "

"There's nobody like that here!" she snapped, cutting him off. But at that precise moment, the deputy caught a glimpse of movement over her shoulder. Someone was peeking at him from around the corner of a wall.

"You there! Step out!"

Realizing he had been discovered, Butch Striker showed himself. The camouflage jacket he'd been wearing earlier had been swapped for a faded orange sweatshirt to look as if he'd been complying with deer hunting regulations.

"What are you harassing my family for?" Striker shouted from behind the old woman. "We ain't done nothing wrong. Go arrest some poachers and leave us alone!"

"This isn't harassment, it's an investigation," Gaydos said. Then, feeling a bit odd that he was speaking through a glass door, he added, "I want you to step out here and show me some identification."

Striker shoved open the door and went outside, the two men becoming dark silhouettes under a low, silver moon. Striker, in his mid-thirties, stood six foot four and possessed the gaunt, ruddy look of a heavy drinker. His hair, the color of surface rust on metal, had been pulled back into a long ponytail that fell below his shoulders. "What's this all about?" Striker demanded, his voice making the question sound more like a threat.

Gaydos, old enough to be the man's father, refused to let Striker bully him. "You know exactly what it's all about," he said. "You were trespassing on posted property and hunting without orange — you and whoever was on the back of your four-wheeler."

"That was my wife," Striker growled. "And I got orange on!"

"Now you do. But you didn't before. Neither did your wife. And you almost ran me over back at the — "

Striker cut him off, his face turning beat red. "Hold on a minute! I didn't know you were a game warden, man. I thought you were the landowner."

And I'm wearing a Mickey Mouse outfit instead of a green uniform with a badge pinned to my chest, thought Gaydos.

In typical outlaw fashion, Striker had an excuse for everything. And Gaydos knew that when he ran out of lies his next move would be either to flee or to fight. Unsnapping his portable radio, Gaydos keyed the mike and called in his location, requesting backup.

"Hey! What are you doing that for?"

Gaydos ignored the question. "Do you have a hunting license, Mr. Striker?"

"Yeah, I got one."

"I want to see it."

Striker turned his back, briefly displaying a hunting license pinned to his sweatshirt before spinning around to face the deputy once more.

Gaydos shook his head wearily. "I want you to take your hunting license out of its holder and hand it over to me."

Striker fell into a momentary trance, his eyes dark and brooding. "I ain't showing you nothing, man. You got that? Now, get off my property!"

"You need to reconsider that," Gaydos said evenly, "because the only one going anywhere will be you heading for the poky if you don't start cooperating."

Striker cocked his head and smiled. The old man had guts! What's more, he believed him. He wheeled around to show his license again. "Go ahead, my man. Take it."

Butch Striker seemed to change from easygoing to explosive like a lion on the Serengeti Plain. So it was with caution that Gaydos removed his hunting license from its plastic holder and copied down the information needed for a citation. "I see the big game tag is missing."

"It's on the deer I killed, just like it's supposed to be. You must have heard the shot. I left the carcass lying near the trail where you stopped me."

"You mean, where I *tried* to stop you."

"C'mon, man . . . I told you I didn't know you were a game warden. Look, you saw my license; now I just want to go and get my deer. Okay?"

Gaydos wasn't about to let Striker out of his sight. "Plenty of time for that," he said. "Besides, Wasserman is on his way. When he gets here you can ask him about it."

"Is that who you called on your radio before — Wasserman?"

"That's right."

Striker's lips pressed into a thin white line. "Yeah, I've heard all about the guy. Why did you have to bring *him* into this?"

"Because up until now, you've been uncooperative."

"What are you talking about? I never gave you a hard time!"

Gaydos could sense one of Butch Striker's mood swings looming, and tried to calm him down. "Wasserman is going to ask you a few questions about the deer," he said, "see if you had permission to be on your neighbor's property — that sort of thing. Relax. No big deal."

"Yeah, well it's a big deal to me, pal. You already asked me a bunch of questions." The veins in Strikers neck began to swell like thick cords of steel. His face a dark scowl. "You should have left him out of this. I want my deer before the coyotes drag it off, and I ain't' waiting around for Wasserman or anybody else!"

When deputy Gaydos radioed for backup, stating he was with Butch Striker, my heart skipped a beat. Striker was a ticking time bomb known for his aggressive antisocial behavior and random fits of violence. And it was a well-known fact that he hated law enforcement officers.

I hung up my mike, slammed my Ford Bronco into passing gear, and watched the speedometer climb past 100 before finally leveling off. *God, please don't let a deer run out in front of me now*. The night had turned black as coal, visibility poor, but the highway was a long straight shot, and fortunately, the only vehicle on it was mine.

Seconds passed like minutes as I raced toward Gaydos, my guts churning with sickening apprehension. *Tamarack Road*, he had said. S*eventh house on left*.

There! Just ahead. A paved state road cutting to my right. I slammed my brakes and turned in.

But it was already too late: Gaydos fell to the ground; his head snapping back and hitting a rock as he collapsed under Striker's vicious right cross. The outlaw quickly straddled him, pummeling him, his fists slamming into the lawman's skull like mindless pile drivers. In the dark, he couldn't see the deputy's face, eyes rolled back into his head. Or could he? — and just wanted to finish the job for good!

I shook the nightmare out of my head. No way! My deputy was too experienced to let that happen to him. *But it's always the experienced snake handler that's bitten, isn't it, Bill?* whispered the nagging voice trapped inside my skull. And I felt a trickle of sweat roll down the center of my back.

First house! Second! I mentally counted as my Bronco shot down Tamarack Road. In the distance, I spotted my deputy's truck. One hundred yards and I'd be there. My eyes strained through the darkness, hoping to catch a glimpse of him — hoping my nightmare hadn't come true. I ground the Bronco to a shuddering stop behind his pickup, my heart racing.

There! On the front porch, two silhouettes: one my deputy, the other, Butch Striker.

Gaydos turned toward me and waved. I heaved a huge sigh of relief. He started toward my vehicle, and I quickly exited the Bronco. "Gene, are you all right?" I breathed as we met on Striker's lawn.

Gaydos shook his head wearily. "This guy is a real psycho. Calm one minute, and the next minute he's in your face like a bad dream."

"Speaking of bad dreams . . ." I began. Then, thinking better of it — "Never mind. Glad you're okay. What's going on with Striker?"

Gaydos brought me up to date while Striker rocked on the balls of his feet and glanced nervously from us to his ATV and back again.

"Some people never learn," I said when Gaydos finished talking. "I'm not surprised he ran on you, either. Would have expected nothing less from a member of the Striker clan."

Gaydos nodded in agreement. "You should have seen him wheel that ATV around those trees. He can really — "

"Wait a minute!" I cut in. "Did you tell him he could leave?"

Gaydos pivoted on his heels, saw Striker heading for his four-wheeler. "No! I told him to stay put."

Lean and athletic, Striker moved across his yard in the long, rapid steps of an African racing ostrich. I called out, ordering him to stop, but he never broke stride.

I tore after him, reaching Striker just as he jumped on his ATV and cranked it up. "Shut it down!" I cried, blocking his path. "Shut it down, now!"

Striker started wrenching back on the hand throttle, revving the engine menacingly. The sound was deafening, and for a moment, I thought he might run me down. But he must have read my face, knew I wouldn't let him pass, because he suddenly killed the engine, leaped to the ground, and came charging at me.

"Who do you think you are, telling me what to do on my own property!" he shrieked. His eyes burned with hatred, hands closed into tight fists.

He was on top of me so fast I barely had time to react. My arms shot forward like two battering rams, palms slamming into his chest as I put my entire body into the blow. Striker reeled backwards and tumbled clumsily over his four-wheeler, limbs flailing wildly as he crashed to the ground.

I unsnapped my handcuffs and started after him. Striker jumped to his feet and came at me again, his face wild with rage. Gaydos had closed in fast. I moved to the left, giving the deputy room, hoping the two of us could bring Striker down long enough to snap on my cuffs. But Striker saw he was outnumbered and stopped dead in his tracks. "I'll kill both of you!" he roared. "You no good — "

He never finished his last word. Two women came charging across the lawn at us, screaming like banshees. One, the elderly woman who had met Gaydos at the door, the other, Striker's wife. They grabbed him from behind, latched onto him, smothered him as they pulled and tugged at his body trying to draw him away from Gaydos and me.

For a moment, I was taken aback. What now? Did I have to wade through these two howling women in order to make an arrest? And then what? Risk injuring one or both of them over what started out as a minor game law infraction?

Then from the corner of my eye, I saw a sudden flash of light to my left. I looked quickly. Striker's neighbor was taking a video recording of the melee, the brilliant light of his camera unmistakable in the black of night. Butch Striker saw it too and shrieked at the man to shut off his camera as he fought to free himself from the two women.

The light went out as quickly as it appeared, and I turned back just in time to see another figure coming at us. It was the old man who had been sitting at the kitchen table when Gaydos came to the door — Striker's father. Waving a stout cane over his head, the obese man hobbled forward at an astonishing pace. "I'm gonna bash your brains out!" he screamed as he zeroed in on me.

With my attention momentarily drawn toward his father, Striker lashed out and struck me in the chin with his fist while his wife and his mother hung desperately to him. Fortunately, I saw it coming and pulled back, sustaining nothing more than a glancing blow.

Realizing what her husband had just done, Striker's wife looked at me with horror in her eyes. She pushed her back into him and faced me, arms spread protectively like wings. His elderly mother and father joined her, cradling their son, making it impossible to take Striker without the likelihood of injuring them.

Although the matter had evolved far beyond a petty game law violation — striking a police officer is a felony — I was reluctant to risk physical injury to Striker's elderly parents — both of whom were considerably overweight with possible health conditions, and the father at least partially disabled.

Hoping against all reason that I might get his family to voluntarily back off, I barked a warning: "Striker, you're under arrest! Tell your family to step aside or they'll be going to jail along with —"

Sirens! Two cars, one emitting a long undulating wail, the other a sharp *whoop-whoop-whoop,* were closing in on us fast. The Strikers froze in their tracks, and I watched shoulders sag and jaws slacken as the chaotic wailing grew louder with each passing second.

Suddenly we saw the pulsating flash of red emergency lights burst through the night in great, blinding strokes. Two police vehicles rolled to a stop behind my Bronco. Doors flew open and three state troopers spread into a marching fan of gray uniforms as they advanced.

Striker's father backed away from his son, followed quickly by the two women. Butch Striker suddenly stood alone, frozen in the center of his lawn. Finally realizing the seriousness of their circumstances, they stood blinking in utter dumb dismay at the sudden show of force.

Having worked with the state police many times over the years, I knew each officer by name: Troopers Tom Sheridan, Mark Lavelle, and John Suhanich surrounded Butch Striker and his family — a clan they had grown accustomed to over the years. Sheridan was first to speak: "How many are we taking with us, Bill?" he said.

I looked at Striker's mother for a moment, then shifted my gaze to his father, and then to his wife . . . and saw not hatred and rage in their eyes, but rather sadness and apprehension. My bitterness quickly faded as I realized they were merely trying to constrain Striker, and, in the best way they knew how, keep him from going to jail.

"Butch Striker is under arrest for assaulting an officer," I said to Sheridan. Then added, "Charges on the rest of these people are pending."

Truth is, and probably always will be, that some folks can't accept the fact that state game wardens are actually police officers commissioned with the same power of arrest that any other police officer has. This lack of comprehension often makes the wildlife enforcement officer's job difficult at best. The Strikers fell into this category of obliviousness, and had it not been for a neighbor dialing 911 to alert the state police, the incident would most certainly have deteriorated into an all-out brawl.

After handcuffing Striker, we placed him into a patrol car and took him to the state police barracks in Tunkhannock where he was fingerprinted and moved to a cell while Trooper Sheridan and I prepared criminal felony assault and misdemeanor charges against him. We also incorporated charges of resisting inspection and failure to wear orange clothing while deer hunting.

District Justice Patricia Robinson drove to the barracks that night and arraigned Striker. Bail was set at $30,000, which got Striker a free trip to jail, where he sat for several days until signing off his house, barn, and shed as security with a bondsman.

Striker appeared in court seven weeks later represented by a high-priced attorney out of Scranton. Rather than slog through a long trial, the district attorney struck a plea bargain deal with Striker, and the matter was settled that day when he pled guilty to everything but the felony assault charge, resulting in a $3000 fine plus eight years revocation of his hunting privileges. Additional attorney fees set him back another grand.

I didn't have a problem with the plea deal. After all, what had started as a relatively minor offense (albeit a very important safety regulation — hunting without fluorescent orange) turned into a disaster for Butch Striker.

Had he stopped for Deputy Gaydos when signaled, his fine would have been $100 without the likelihood of revocation. But Striker chose to flee. And when confronted by Gaydos, he became uncooperative, his hostile behavior erupting to the point that additional officers had to be called in. As a result, Striker's willful disregard for wildlife laws and the officers who enforce them, had cost him dearly.

Two Years Later.

Deer season means long days of endless hours on patrol and many sleepless nights for most game wardens — and this year was no exception. My radio blared constantly as the dispatcher at regional headquarters reported an endless string of violations-in-progress to officers in a dozen neighboring counties. My own district in Wyoming County was no exception; I had been on the go since long before daylight, and it was approaching dark when I spotted an old Buick parked along a narrow back road bordering the woods.

Easing my Bronco to a crawl, I pulled up behind the Buick and stopped. I could see a single figure sitting in the driver's seat. He was peering fixedly into the woods through an open window, his gaze so ambitious he never noticed as I walked to his vehicle from the opposite side and looked in at him.

Noticeably overweight, his white hair cut short but unkempt, he wore a heavy, red and white checkered shirt and thick woolen trousers. A knurled wooden cane lay on the seat next to him, the curved handle worn smooth from years of frequent use. Across his lap rested the business end of a high-powered rifle.

"State game warden," I called through the open passenger window.

The old man whipped his head around in utter surprise. Then he stared straight into my eyes, his face lined with worry. "Wasserman!" he murmured. His expression a mixture of apprehension and contempt.

He looked vaguely familiar to me, but I couldn't remember where I had met him before. "See any deer?" I asked.

"I ain't hunting. Just looking."

It was the usual answer that I got from every road hunter I came across. "I'd like to see your hunting license and some identification."

"License should be in my glove box," he offered hesitantly. I was impressed that he knew not to reach into a concealed compartment without my permission.

I nodded toward the dashboard. "Go ahead . . ."

He stretched across the seat with a low groan, popped open the glove box, and pulled out a state issued hunting license. Snapping the lid closed with a flick of his wrist he said, "Driver's license is in my wallet; guess you want to see that too."

I nodded. "Yes, sir."

The old man cracked open his door. "Coming out!" he grunted. After pulling himself off the seat with considerable effort, he stood by the open door and sucked in a series of deep labored breaths.

"Are you okay?" I asked.

He nodded he was and shambled around the Buick, pushing against its frame with his hand for support until he finally stood before me.

"Don't recognize me, do you?" he puffed.

"Should I . . . ?"

He shrugged wearily. "It was dark that night. Too dark to get a good look at me, I guess. I'm Butch Striker's dad. You were at my house a couple years ago."

142

He handed me his hunting license, and the memory of an old man coming at me waving his cane menacingly in the air, came back instantly.

"Ah!" I said.

He was right. I never did get a good look at his face that night. But I sure remembered his name when I was cleaning out my file cabinet a few months later and happened across an old Permit to Hunt from a Vehicle. It had been issued to Gus Striker long before I was assigned to the county.

In those days, anyone with a doctor's letter stating they were permanently unable to walk 25 yards without artificial means of support could be issued such a permit by the Game Commission. But I had seen Gus Striker walk a good 100 feet without using his cane, and it had been all the proof I needed to pull his permit.

And so it was with a cheerful sense of haughty retribution that I wrote a letter to state headquarters in Harrisburg recommending that his permit be revoked.

"Put your wallet away," I said as he dipped into his back pocket. "I remember you now."

The old man regarded me with gray liquid eyes for a long moment. Then he shrugged sadly and spoke: "You took away my permit to hunt from my car. I wish you wouldn't have done that." He took a step backwards and pushed his buttocks against the door of his Buick for support. "Look around!" he gestured with a broad sweep of his hand. "I can't walk into those woods. Even if I shot a deer, I couldn't retrieve it! Walking is too difficult, too painful, — downright impossible some days. And I love to hunt! But you took that away from me when you revoked my permit."

The old man shook his head sorrowfully. "I done wrong that night. I know it. Shouldn't have come at you like I did. But I was scared for my boy." He shrugged a heavy shoulder, turned his head, and gazed into the woods. Nightfall was close at hand, the descending darkness adding to Striker's somber mood. "Guess that's not much of an excuse," he said softly, "but it's the truth sure enough."

I felt immediate pity for the man. There was no doubt in my mind that Gus Striker could not walk very far without risking his health. Perhaps he'd managed it on pure adrenalin the night we were at his house. But today I saw a sad and broken man who could barely climb out of his car let alone take a leisurely stroll in the woods.

Suddenly I remembered the vindictive glee I had felt as I initiated the process that would ultimately result in Gus Striker losing his permit, and I was ashamed. I had always taken pride not to allow my personal feelings to interfere with my job, but failed to live up to that vital standard when it came to Gus Striker. He might have been able to walk the minimum 25-yard requirement without using a cane, but at what expense? Bodily injury from a fall — or a heart attack, perhaps?

I handed the old man his hunting license. He stuffed it into his pants pocket. "So now what?" he said. "Gonna arrest me?"

I turned and looked up and down the lonesome back road. "I don't see any signs that say 'No Parking' around here. Do you?"

The old man eyed me curiously for a moment. Then he pushed himself off his Buick and started around the car in awkward, plodding steps.

"Mr. Striker," I called.

He turned and stared back at me in silence.

"Have your doctor send me a letter. I'll get you a new permit."

IT HAD BEEN a year since my encounter with Gus Striker, and I was surprised to find him on the other end of my phone, but even more surprising was the reason for his call:

In a gruff and matter-of-fact tone of voice, the old man proceeded to tell me about a group of poachers who were killing game over bait in a wooded area near his home. "It's a big operation," he said. "They're wiping out all the game. Ain't nothing left to shoot at no more." He hesitated for a while, his breathing labored and shallow. "You done something for me once," he remarked. "Now I'm returning the favor. After this, we're even. You won't hear from me again."

He hung up and I sat listening to the low hum of the disconnected line in stunned silence. Of all the people in the world, Gus Striker was last on my list of people who I thought would ever call me about a game law violation. And although I'd had my share of informants over the years — some with good information and some bad — there was no doubt in my mind that Striker was on the level.

And as it turned out, his information had been extremely accurate, ushering me into one of the biggest poaching rings of my career, and enabling me to put an end to a gang of local outlaws that had been participating in the systematic and ruthless slaughter of innocent wildlife for decades.

Acknowledgements

I would like to thank my beautiful wife, Marianne, for the endless hours she endured listening to me babble on about the different stories in the book, and for her encouragement and help in bringing my manuscript to fruition.

Thanks to my twin brother, John, for artfully designing my book covers over the years, helping me with the interior photographs, and for proofreading my manuscripts.

Thanks to Andy Mazzanti for your friendship, patriotism, and your keen eye in proofreading the book.

Thanks to Lisa Mazzanti for coming to the rescue, so that I could get my books formatted properly over the years.

Thanks to Deputy Gene Gaydos and Deputy Jeff Pierce for your friendship and your untiring dedication to our wildlife resources. You were always there when I needed you.

Thanks to my friend Ed Bond, Game Protector Extraordinaire, who taught me to have empathy toward others and to enforce the law with proper decorum.

About the Author

William Wasserman started his career with the Pennsylvania Game Commission in 1974 and retired after 32 years of dedicated service. Wasserman is a prolific writer who has been published in dozens of national magazines including *Black Belt, Fur-Fish-Game, Pennsylvania Game News, International Game Warden, South Carolina Wildlife,* and *The Alberta Game Warden*. He also penned a weekly outdoor newspaper column for 15 years, and hosted a popular outdoor talk-radio program for eight years. He has written five books about his life as a state game warden.

About the Author